SPORTS BUSINESS
UNPLUGGED

Leadership Challenges
from the World of Sports

Rick Burton and Norm O'Reilly

Foreword by David Stern

Syracuse University Press

SUPPORT FROM SYRACUSE UNIVERSITY'S DAVID B. FALK COLLEGE OF
SPORT AND HUMAN DYNAMICS TOWARD THE PRODUCTION OF THIS BOOK
IS GRATEFULLY ACKNOWLEDGED.

ALL AUTHOR PROCEEDS WILL BENEFIT STUDENT SCHOLARSHIPS AT THE
AUTHORS' RESPECTIVE SCHOOLS.

Library of Congress Cataloging-in-Publication Data
Names: Burton, Rick, author. | O'Reilly, Norm, 1973– author.
Title: Sports business unplugged : leadership challenges from the world of
    sports / Rick Burton and Norm O'Reilly ; foreword by David Stern.
Description: First edition. | Syracuse, New York : Syracuse University
    Press, 2016. | Includes index.
Identifiers: LCCN 2016014359| ISBN 9780815634768 (pbk. : alk. paper)
    | ISBN 9780815653929 (e-book)
Subjects: LCSH: Sports—Economic aspects. | Sports administration.
Classification: LCC GV716 .B86 2016 | DDC 338.47796—dc23 LC
    record available at https://lccn.loc.gov/2016014359

Contents

Illustrations

Tables

Foreword

IT IS NOT OFTEN that magazines or newspapers covering the sports industry have the luxury of employing former league commissioners or national Olympic team advisers for their regular bylines. But that's exactly what *SportsBusiness Journal* (*SBJ*) discovered when it began to use regular opinion columns from university professors Rick Burton and Norm O'Reilly.

Rick, an old friend from my first year as commissioner of the National Basketball Association (NBA), had ably served as the commissioner of Australia's National Basketball League, and Dr. Norm O'Reilly had worked on numerous projects for the Canadian Olympic Committee. When they joined forces in 2009 (Rick at Syracuse University and Norm initially at Syracuse and now at Ohio University) and began writing regular columns for *SBJ*, they brought a unique insight to their observations.

Not only could they combine familiarity with the practitioner side of our industry, but they could also apply a research orientation that reflected their combined time in the "ivory tower." Don't get me wrong, I use the term *ivory tower* not to diminish the value of academicians but to suggest that someone not living in the day to day of the sports industry can actually take the time to reflect holistically on what is happening. And that's what Rick and Norm did on a near monthly basis. I cannot emphasize enough how important such a "dual" perspective is when analyzing our industry, and I believe the readers of *SBJ* have benefited. I know I certainly have.

To that end, all of the columns you will find reprinted in this book ran in *SBJ* over the past seven years and have offered tremendous value to practitioners and students alike. But what I have always liked about Burton and O'Reilly's work is that their commentary is never dated or out of touch. In fact, as I go back through the columns they have selected for inclusion in the book, I see added value that I certainly missed the first time around.

I would emphasize again that these columns offer huge value for practitioners and future practitioners in sport. As our industry continues to grow and formalize, I know firsthand that knowledge, learning, and competitive edge are vital not only at the league and club level but also at the individual level for those seeking promotions or entry as professionals into our complex field.

We all know that knowledge is power, and these columns offer great advantages to those who take the time to read them.

I encourage your consideration of the content shared in this book and hope you will enjoy some of the fine writing that graces the pages of the sports industry's leading trade journal.

David Stern
NBA Commissioner Emeritus

1. National Basketball Association commissioner David Stern (1984–2014). *Courtesy of the National Basketball Association.*

Acknowledgments

WE WOULD LIKE to note the support and help of a number of wonderful people in the publishing of this book. Without them, this book doesn't exist.

At Syracuse University Press

- Suzanne Guiod, editor in chief; Alice Randel Pfeiffer, director; Vicky Lane, senior book designer; Mona Hamlin, marketing analyst; Brendan Missett, project editor; Kelly Balenske, assistant editor; and Deb Manion, acquisitions editor; as well as our copy editor in New Mexico, Annie Barva

At Syracuse University

- Chancellor Kent Syverud, Falk College dean Diane Lyden Murphy, Sue Cornelius Edson, Margie Chetney, Renee Crown Honors Program director Steve Kuusisto, Hoang-Anh Tran, Falk College Department of Sport Management director Michael Veley, Michele Jachim Barrett, David Salanger, Gabe Nugent (in the General Counsel's Office), and sport management graduate assistant Aaron Rudy

At Ohio University

- Dean Hugh Sherman, Jess Storm Steele, Michael Stephens, Ben Siegel, Jennifer Daniels, and Jessica Gardner

At *SportsBusiness Journal*

- Richard Weiss, publisher; Abe Madkour, executive editor; and the steward who selected and edited these columns, the very wonderful Betty Gomes

At the National Hockey League
 • Commissioner Gary Bettman, Jessica Johnson, and Melynda Pilon for the contribution of beautiful color photos

At the Atlantic Coast Conference
 • Commissioner John Swofford and Amy Yakola

At the National Basketball Association
 • Joseph Amati, Linda Tosi, and Emma Zingone

Our families
 • Barb, Stephanie, Andrew (particularly for his great photos), and Meredith Burton
 • Nadege, Emma, Kian, Thomas, and Leland O'Reilly

Our mentors
 • David Stern, former National Basketball Association commissioner and the provider of a wonderful foreword
 • Dick Pound, International Olympic Committee member and former World Anti-Doping Agency president and IOC marketing vice president
 • George Foster, Stanford University Graduate School of Business Management professor
 • Gene Laczniak, Marquette University marketing professor

And in particular
 • Gary Pasqualicchio, the graduate assistant at Ohio University who helped us pull all the manuscript pieces together and worked so closely with Syracuse University Press to ensure we hit deadlines and turned things in the right way

Abbreviations

AFL	Australian Football League
AHL	American Hockey League
BOCOG	Beijing Organizing Committee for the Olympic Games
CAGR	compounded annual growth rate
CBA	Collective Bargaining Agreement
CFL	Canadian Football League
CFO	chief financial officer
CIS	Canadian Interuniversity Sport
CMO	chief marketing officer
COC	Canadian Olympic Committee
COO	chief operating officer
CPC	Canadian Paralympic Committee
CPM	cost per thousand
CSLS	Canadian Sponsorship Landscape Study
EPL	English Premier League
F1	Formula One
FIFA	Fédération Internationale de Football Association
IAAF	International Association of Athletics Federation
IF	international federation
IOC	International Olympic Committee
IPL	Indian Premier League
KHL	Kontinental Hockey League
MLB	Major League Baseball
MLS	Major League Soccer
MOOC	massive open online course

NASCAR   National Association for Stock Car Auto Racing
NBA   National Basketball Association
NCAA   National Collegiate Athletics Association
NFL   National Football League
NFLPA   National Football League Players' Association
NGB   national governing body
NHL   National Hockey League
NHLPA   National Hockey League Players' Association
NL   National League
ROI   return on investment
SBJ   *SportsBusiness Journal*
SMA   Sport Marketing Association
TOP   The Olympic Program
UEFA   Union of European Football Associations
UFC   Ultimate Fighting Championship
U.N.   United Nations
USOC   U.S. Olympic Committee
VANOC   Vancouver Organizing Committee
WADA   World Anti-Doping Agency
WNBA   Women's National Basketball Association
YOG   Youth Olympic Games

Introduction

IN 2009, the two of us began writing monthly columns for our friends at *SportsBusiness Journal*—affectionately known as "*SBJ*" in the North American sports industry. At first, the opportunity to write for *SBJ* and our many acquaintances in the sports world was a bit of a dream, but neither of us imagined that seven years later we would have written more than 60 opinion or insight pieces on an economic sector that we follow closely, work in continually, and teach about daily. The number of positive comments we've received and conversations we've started is something we've often discussed, and we're proud these columns have resonated with industry professionals and students alike.

The *SBJ* pieces compose one of a number of projects we have partnered on over the years. We write together on projects outside of *SBJ* and have done academic papers for scholarly journals, but we also recently published a textbook titled *Global Sport Marketing: Sponsorship, Ambush Marketing, and the Olympic Games* (2015), alongside IOC member and renowned author Richard Pound and two fellow academics, Benoit Seguin and Michelle Brunette. This kind of frequent interaction and partnership has built an innate sense of timing for us—like a shortstop and second baseman combining on a double play or a point guard and a power forward executing a pick and roll. Or, to fit with our often Olympic theme, the third runner on the 4×100 relay smoothly executing the curve and a baton pass to the anchor, who takes it home for the team. Now, we wouldn't want to say that we finish each other's sentences (just yet!), but we have become remarkably fluent in gauging what the other thinks and building on our individual experiences to share what we believe to be a highly valuable column. As in one of our favorite sports, ice hockey, we see things as the crisp pass that snaps off one stick and glues itself to the next before a sure shot finds the back of the net!

The impetus for this book came from industry contacts, *SBJ*, and our colleagues. However, the most important drivers for both of us were our current and future students. Both of us have taught in a number of places and are currently working in two great sport management institutions: Syracuse University and Ohio University. As the number of programs in our growing (and formalizing) field continues to climb (now estimated at more than 1,000 globally), several institutions have emerged as leaders in our field, including Syracuse (where we began collaborating as faculty members in 2009) and Ohio (our field's oldest program and one that will turn an astounding 50 years old in 2016–17).

The interest we've received from our students and their engagement is the number one reason we've pursued this book and hope to continue to write for *SBJ* for many years to come. For this book specifically, we wanted to use material that felt timeless or consistently worth discussing (particularly since history has a nasty habit of repeating itself). So, after looking at more than six years of material and working closely with Syracuse University Press and *SBJ*, we have compiled an assortment of columns that ran from 2009 to 2015.

During that era, the sports world evolved rapidly in response to new ideas, new technology, enhanced competition, and new media platforms. The biggest properties (such as the IOC, FIFA, the NFL, NHL, UEFA, NBA, MLB, NCAA, UFC, NASCAR and others) gave us Vancouver 2010, Super Bowls, London 2012, Sochi 2014, two World Cups, Stanley Cups, world championships and national champions. All of those mega-events and numerous marketing or management initiatives gave us monthly leeway to comment on what we believed our industry should acknowledge or leverage. We were able to go beyond many of these mainstream ideas and inform industry leaders (*SBJ*'s readers) about the role that sports plays in a healthy (and equal) society and in communities of all sizes and colors around the world.

If someone once said the revolution is coming . . . our approach has been that the evolution (of sports) is ongoing, ever expanding, deeply engaging, and never less than interesting.

We hope you will find our observations cogent, and, as always, if we have touched a nerve or said something you agree with, we would love to hear from you. Our email addresses have traditionally followed each of our columns, so our collective work has always been open for immediate feedback. We have never hidden behind anything we wrote and welcome your comments at rhburton@syr.edu and oreillyn@ohio.edu.

As many in our industry know, we are quick to respond, keen to discuss and happy to provide our research or engage students in projects to help all of us make sport better.

Rick Burton and Norm O'Reilly
February 2016

SPORTS BUSINESS UNPLUGGED

PART ONE

Marketing and Sponsorship

1

Can More Sponsors Seize the Day, and the Activation?

Published October 5, 2015

IF YOU'RE A PRO HOCKEY FAN or just a good old-fashioned sports marketer, you probably heard about last year's sponsorship excitement involving a young goaltender playing for the NHL's Ottawa Senators. Don't tell us you missed it. Even our respective students thought it was "epic."

Andrew Hammond, a then 27-year-old who played his college hockey at Bowling Green, was finally getting his chance to play in the NHL. Interestingly, he had decided to carry the nickname Hamburglar, which many people over 40 might recognize as the McDonald's cartoon character fictitiously immortalized for stealing hamburgers.

Hammond didn't steal sandwiches. He stole goals from opposing players. And the Ottawa fans soon loved him for it. By chance, McDonald's was a sponsor of the Senators. So there you have it. A player's nickname was catchy and fun (not to mention his helmet graphics were cool) . . . and then something even more unusual went down.

Hammond responded to a late-season call-up to the Senators by going 17-1-1 in his first 19 starts, which (incredibly) led to the greatest comeback run by a team making the playoffs in NHL history. Hammond's performances electrified a fan base that had not seen much to cheer about since a 2007 run to the Stanley Cup Final. Simply put, the Hamburglar's brilliance led to pandemonium in Ottawa and high interest in the professional hockey world.

So good was Hammond's run that Ottawa fans were reported to have started eating McDonald's burgers pregame to keep his streak alive, while others threw them on the ice after games and still more started filling social media with mentions and re-mentions of both McDonald's and Hammond.

As reported by Don Brennan in the *Ottawa Sun*, McDonald's took notice when Hammond picked up a hamburger that a fan threw on the ice and saluted the crowd with it. Moving like an entrepreneur, the burger giant awarded the Hamburglar with McDonald's food for life.

This is a sponsor that was able to turn something as mundane as a hockey player's nickname and convert it into a sponsorship activation. This is about a big bureaucratic sponsor that moved quickly enough to capitalize on an unpredictable streak that could've stopped at any moment.

We acknowledge that McDonald's was an official Senators sponsor, which helped the situation come to life. But, unquestionably, McDonald's was either prepared for the opportunity or knew how to move on a market opportunity. This ability seems pretty rare in conservative companies, and when we see it, we have to give the company props.

"When an opportunity like this develops naturally on its own, it's incumbent on a pro team and sponsor to be aware of the environment and act quickly if they are going to capitalize on the activation," Cyril Leeder, president of the Senators, told us. "McDonald's moved swiftly, and this was only possible because of our long-standing [and] strong partnership with them. I am not sure we could have acted as quickly, or as effectively, with one of our newer partners."

What Leeder said next was also interesting as it relates to fan avidity and knowledge of the fan base.

"The Hamburglar activation resonated with all of our fans, young and old. He's a character many of our baby boomers recognized and loved, and his appearance in the arena and throughout the community added significantly to Hamburglarmania in Ottawa," Leeder said. "But give the McDonald's activation and sponsorship team credit for recognizing the opportunity and acting on it so quickly."

Recognition of the fans and decisive speed cause us to cite an academic example about coaching that one of us worked on years ago. The premise was that managing in baseball was about picking the right players and hoping they would make the right plays in the field. In football, the coaches needed to pick the right players and the right plays, and then tell the players exactly what to do. Players weren't required to think as much as they needed to know the playbook and execute the play the coach called in from the sideline.

Today, coaching has changed. Modern management reflects the fast-paced, instant decision-making of basketball and soccer. Here, the coach needs to instill in his or her players the ability to think and react quickly. A coach might draw up a play for Sally to shoot the ball, but if she's guarded, Sally needs to create something on the fly and engage Sue and Stephanie ad hoc.

McDonald's created a brilliant activation that made us ponder whether sponsorship managers are nimble enough for the 2020s. Should sponsorship contracts at the club, league, player or event level allow for environmental luck? How can activations be adapted as on-the-fly perceptions, discussions and social posts change in content, tone and popularity? Do they have a "Sally" proactively ready to act, or an engaged "Sue" to respond? Are digital and experiential teams aligned and integrated?

We ask to consider if partnership agreements have gotten so fixated on managing the specific details of the contract that the sudden big idea is no longer possible with modern sponsorship. Has contemporary marketing become nothing more than determining who has the biggest wallet or the most guts to buy the property assets with the greatest reach?

Or can the odd Hamburglar moment exist in FIFA, the Olympic Games and the NFL?

2

Space: The Next Frontier in Sports Sponsorship?

Published November 24, 2014

"SORRY. That table is taken, but I can offer you one on the patio." This is something we often heard after arriving at a popular restaurant on a jam-packed day when we showed up without a reservation. It's not what we wanted to learn but might end up giving us a premium we didn't expect.

After hearing the news that Ford has entered into a sponsorship agreement that includes rights to the outdoor space around the Air Canada Centre in the heart of Toronto (Canada's largest city and North America's fifth largest), we wondered if this new direction had hit other forms of sponsorship as well.

Ford's announcement, reportedly after fan objections to the automaker's unfortunate similarity with Toronto's controversial Mayor Rob Ford, was part of an initially announced plan to change the name of Maple Leaf Square to Ford Square. That ultimately led to Ford Fan Zone at Maple Leaf Square, and that piqued our curiosity further.

It provides evidence that a corporation sees significant value in such a public-facing investment. Much like the condo market (where the air above condos is bought and sold), the air and space near major sporting venues and clubs is suddenly accruing value.

Or, perhaps it is not the space itself that has any value but the platform it provides for activation to reach a particular target market who uses that space regularly (residents of the area) or periodically (before and during NHL, NBA, or MLB playoff runs).

As professors of sponsorship, we wondered if the e-textbooks of 2020 will show a sports marketing mix that includes the air and space option alongside traditional contra provisions, cash-back guarantees, interchangeable naming rights and self-liquidating variable/dynamic ticket sales promotions.

We imagine there are many others. What about sponsoring the parking spots of star players or the hangar and reception area for a team's private airplane? How about sponsoring the physical (or digital) highway that leads from the nearest airport to the team's stadium?

Some of those are hard to imagine, but if you really think about it, these kinds of concepts make sense and reflect the evolutionary nature of sponsorship. The long-standing flexibility of this marketing tactic underpins so many strategies and revenue schemes.

Very specifically, it is getting harder to reach people in places where they are actually paying attention and to leverage them in situations where they might listen to new ideas or associate their team loyalty with future consumer behavior. Clearly, these unique (and scarce) places where high levels of activation are possible will, in our view, continue to grow in value.

Sponsorship, as many have written, is all about activation and opportunities to leverage. And what could be better than activating the space near a high-traffic sports facility where the interior of the building is nothing but restrictions? Or creating concepts that alter perceptions?

Many readers will know that one of us used to work in Sydney and perhaps the most iconic architecture in that fabled city is the Sydney Opera House. If you've never been to Australia, you might expect the Opera House is well-illuminated at night. What might surprise you is learning that the Australians frequently stage art and light shows on the flat-surfaced sails of this spectacular building.

To that end, think about how the Ford logo dominates the roof of Ford Field in Detroit. Those aerial shots from someone's tire or insurance blimp now give much more bang for Ford's sponsorship buck.

Want another way of thinking about this point? Let's do a pop quiz: What's the first thing that comes to mind if we write the phrase "Levi's Stadium in San Francisco"? For many it will not be about work jeans but rather a lengthy discussion about the gargantuan commitment to technology and network interconnectivity.

Not far away in Sacramento, the Kings are rapidly leveraging a "farm-to-fork" concept that reportedly will guarantee 90 percent of the team's food and drink will be locally sourced within 150 miles of Sacramento's new arena (opening in October 2016). That supposedly means more than 740 farmers will be producing beef, pork, poultry, cheeses, olive oil, craft beers and wines for the food and beverage patrons of the Kings' future home.

The theme to the two examples: Contemporary sports marketers are aggressively pushing the envelope and getting better at thinking outside the traditional sponsorship circle that has long relied on signage and VIP suites.

To that end, why not think about space and spatial designs in new ways? If you go back and review the history of mathematics, you'll learn that, at one time, zero and negative numbers didn't exist. They were heretical (so to speak). Then someone said "zero" was possible.

Might allow us to wonder what new concepts can be shaped for sponsorship in the coming decades and whether there is air out there that is waiting to be sold.

3

Benefits of Long-Term Sports Partnership Worth Going "All In"

Published September 8, 2014

TWO MAJOR PLAYERS in the sports industry—Nike and NBCUniversal—have made significant, decades-long investments in content they clearly value and did so at a time when many industry experts are hesitant to look much beyond 2020.

On those grounds, these organizations appear to have pushed a lot of poker chips into the middle of the table. Said another way, they went "all in"—and "all in" for a while.

The cards as we see them? Nike's agreement to invest a reported half a billion dollars in USA Track & Field to lock up exclusive sponsorship rights until the year 2040, followed by Comcast's NBCUniversal extending its billions-plus television (and media) rights partnership with the IOC until 2032.

It made us ask what Nike and NBC see that their competitors don't? There must be something, right? Given the doping issues of recent years, aging track facilities (in many settings), and a general decline in youth sports participation, is it possible the original Olympic sport of 776 B.C. is actually worth nearly $500 million to Nike? And how about the decision-makers at NBCUniversal? Do they know what they're doing? Allegedly they bid much higher than the expected (or logical) price to make sure they continued to own the Games.

As Vince Lombardi once so famously yelled, "What the hell's going on out here?"

Well, one of the joys of the academic lifestyle is stepping back and thinking about the future . . . as well as the past. And after all gets said and done, we think Nike's leadership and the brain trust at NBCUniversal may have read their fellow card players well.

A recent article in *Sport Management Review* outlined how corporations need to think strategically and formulaically about sponsorship activation (Norm O'Reilly and Denyse Lafrance Horning, November 2013). That may sound elementary, but there are a number of key components to this work, with the most significant finding suggesting that vibrant partnerships happen only if activated appropriately and properly over an extended period of time.

Indeed, there is no magic number to activation (beyond that 2:1 or 3:1 spend ratio that is so often discussed), but there appear to be significant benefits to customized, context-specific, long-term approaches.

So let's note the following: Track and field events do not have the competitive limitations of the major professional team sports at the Olympic Games. In fact, the sport has many different events with elite competitors providing significant profiles in their respective countries. Track and field also works because nearly every country of the world competes, and the cost to participate is often not much more than shoes.

For Nike, a global company, it's nice that the U.S. has historically been the world's top country in track and field. But even if the U.S. falls off, the replacement will be population-rich China. We also note that the IAAF World Athletics Championships are by most accounts the third-largest event in the sporting world, after the Olympics and FIFA World Cup. Names like Michael Johnson, Cathy Freeman, Sergey Bubka, Sebastian Coe, Usain Bolt and many more are known worldwide.

That much makes sense. And having until 2040 is one heck of a runway to leverage or build upon that relationship.

We know that the International Olympic Committee's TOP partners often have grabbed long-term deals (a decade or more), but this is the first time we've seen this (and at this scale) with a national sports organization or national governing body. But maybe Nike's action is an "outlier" move as well as an indicator of things to come. Is it possible more companies will follow the Beaverton, Ore., giant in locking up 25-year deals? Why shouldn't they?

Naming rights for stadiums have frequently gone for multiple decades. In Syracuse, the rumor is that Carrier, the air conditioning manufacturer, did an "in perpetuity" deal for the Carrier Dome (a facility that ironically has no air conditioning), and that stadium is now approaching its 35th year of operation.

That simple thought might suggest longer is better and strong associations over time build better brands.

Look at Coca-Cola's relationship with the Olympics. Coke has been a sponsor without interruption since the 1928 Games in Amsterdam. North of the border, RBC Bank has a similar, near century-long relationship with the Canadian Olympic Committee.

In any of these cases, imagine if they had just done one deal for a short period of time. They could've killed it for four years and then watched a competitor swoop in to take over (or dismantle) the valuable marketing benefits that had accrued.

Maybe this boils down to the notion that if you're planning to activate something important, then lock it up for a good long while. Granted, a sports property can have problems, but long-established sports organizations generally don't get permanently injured, commit crimes or die. So the risk on a long-term investment is probably lower than other property-type deals, such as endorsing athletes, coaches or one-off events.

And that may be the point. If companies are risk-averse, long-term deals should flatten out the variability while providing huge influence in how things are done.

To that end, maybe Nike and NBC are only doing what Coke and RBC learned after World War I ended. That is, if you're dealt an attractive hand (i.e., find an ideal partner with great fit), bet heavily and lock them up. The rewards of a strong partnership are easily worth the risks.

4

Has Experience Trumped Sports in Sponsorship Market?

Published June 17, 2013

IN OUR LAST COLUMN (May 27–June 2), we wrote about North American sponsorship trends and how the partnership landscape is evolving—both in general and for sports, specifically. Our findings suggested notable growth for sponsorship overall but areas of concern for the sports sector.

Our sponsorship and endorsement research led us to another series of questions:

1. Why is sponsorship still growing and continuing to work in a strained economy when marketing budgets are so scrutinized and volatile?

We believe the answer lies very much in the way sports properties view image transfer and its transformative power to benefit non-sports brands. This transfer concept is intuitive to most executives in sports marketing, almost a subliminal given, but much about it is misunderstood, and the concept of true fiscal balance is rarely explored in depth.

Let's create a simplistic example to showcase this. Forgetting for a moment all existing deals, let's suppose the New York Yankees want to sell their soft drink sponsorship rights. We all know they'll want this high-profile category to go for as much money as possible. They'll want a bidding war to break out between Pepsi (which has held the team's rights) and Coke, and anyone else willing to pay the highest premium.

Intuitively, these beverage companies know a deal with the Yankees will connect them to one of the most valuable and recognized sports brands in the world and provide brand-benefiting images of "prestige," "leader," "winner," "high performance" and "superstar." These are adjectives most consumer brands want their positioning to portray, and if product exclusivity comes with the deal, they'll pay a premium. In return for a massive fee (and value-in-kind product), the beverage companies will expect the Yankees to feature the company's signage and pour its products in every team-controlled setting (the stadium, the clubhouse, the VIP boxes, the spring training ballpark, the fantasy camps, etc.).

Let's say that Coke wins. Coke's money will buy brand visibility and exclusive consumption. But what of the aforementioned image transfer? Will the Yankees logo on a Coke bottle drive sales? Will a sign on the center-field scoreboard truly drive awareness, trial or usage by key targets? Will sales of product along the stadium's concourses make this deal truly self-liquidating? Will a luxury box (as part of the deal) facilitate business-to-business initiatives? Even if the answers to those questions (and others) are yes, will the image transfer have better helped the Yankees or Coke?

Will both parties benefit equally in the equation of overall dollars secured vs. ultimate gallons consumed? Perhaps they will, but more often than not, one party will not get as much as it should have. And strangely, often unnoticed in the deal-making, it is the consumer who manages (in his or her subconscious) the actual image transfer.

What we've consistently witnessed is that the real image transfer happens when people experience products firsthand in social environments, and their passion is more connected to their experiential engagement. Said another way: Does a Coke music festival provide a different and more encompassing relationship with the consumer than a Yankees baseball game? If it does, it may explain why sports sponsorship's percentage of the overall partnership pie is slipping.

2. Why are other property types like arts, causes and festivals giving sports a run for its money in sponsorship investments?

We arrived quickly at the issues of servicing (Who does it better?), experiential variability (Are other groups offering better in-sponsorship experiences?) and easier usage of intellectual property. Almost everyone in sports knows how aggressively the NFL and NBA protect their respective brand logos and how difficult it can be to use a sports logo on anything. We fully understand the need for those leagues (and their teams) to take this approach. But in doing so, have they become more difficult than a local festival or charity that is far more relaxed about how the image transfer is facilitated and how sponsors are allowed to activate?

We understand leagues and teams can't go backward in their trademark protection, but if they are stodgy and if non-sport competitors make life easier for the Pepsis of the world, don't for a moment think these "efficiencies" aren't noticed by the entry-level and mid-level manager types who manage sponsorships. They may not negotiate contracts or speak at sponsorship conferences, but they construct frequent reports to bosses on which properties make life easiest.

3. Is there anything sports sponsorship-selling organizations should do differently?

This is a billion-dollar question because sponsorship, according to IEG, is now a $50 billion business worldwide, with sports taking about 50 percent of that pot. That $50 billion is more than double what it was a decade ago, although sports back then was 75 percent of the pie. If sports had kept its share during the past decade, it would have meant billions more poured into our industry.

Does that suggest it's time for sports properties to up the ante on servicing, evaluation, post-sales activations, partner relations and more? Probably. Otherwise, if certain trends continue, future sponsorship numbers may transfer more than a few people out of this image-conscious sports industry.

5

Are Big Numbers Masking Competition for Sponsorship Dollars?

Published May 27, 2013

THERE'S A SONG by Mary Chapin Carpenter called "I Feel Lucky," where she notes in the lyrics that "the stars might lie, but the numbers never do." We wondered if the same axiom held for discussions about sports sponsorship in North America. Is it possible the numbers are lying?

On one hand, the annual IEG pronouncement or the more detailed *Sponsorium Report* (which came out in February) has suggested more money is being spent on sponsorships every year. The Canadian Sponsorship Landscape Study, now collecting data for its extensive seventh edition, says the same and emphasizes sponsorship's growth (up 43 percent since 2006) despite tightened marketing budgets in the post-2008 global banking recession era.

However, this growth in sponsorship is not necessarily the same for sports as it might be for sponsored cause-marketing, festivals/fairs (annual events), concerts, education or the arts. In fact, *Sponsorium* notes the fastest-growing sector of sponsorship was trade shows (up 40 percent) and that sports partnerships were declining in their share of the sponsorship market.

This finding is backed by CSLS, which notes that other areas—primarily festivals (up 12 percent change in 2012 versus 2011)—have been taking a larger chunk of the sports sponsorship's (down 13 percent) slice of the pie. Further, sponsors are telling us (through their actions) that their sweet-spot for ROI is also moving, with festivals tying professional sports as the top source of acceptable ROI for properties, according to the CSLS in 2012. Up to that point, professional sports had always held top billing.

Granted, more money is still spent on sports sponsorships than in any other area, but no one working in sports should neglect the fact that sports' share of the sponsorship investment graph is shrinking. It's a lot like schools and sports clubs a few years back thinking there were no problems with youth physical inactivity and membership rates because there was a bulge created by baby boomers' kids that was hiding certain realities.

In the same way, sponsorship numbers in sports remain healthy and are even growing slightly thanks to the overall growth of sponsorship. But just like sports clubs needed to worry as Gen Xers chose less active lifestyles and didn't back-fill their ranks with offspring, sports properties need to seriously look at arts, festivals, events and causes as their competitors for corporate dollars and creatively up the ante.

But let's be clear. We're not shouting "the sky is falling," but rather we're observing unusual atmospheric conditions.

So here are two questions to consider: Is the current North American sports landscape oversaturated? And, given that the majority of sporting mega-events will take place in other parts of the world for the next decade (Olympics, FIFA World Cup, Rugby World Cup and basketball world championships), is it possible less money will be spent on North American sports (per global capita) than in other parts of the world or even when compared to other forms of sponsorship? Perhaps.

And isn't it possible that in an age of environmental uncertainty, sponsors have been modestly successful at signing long-term contracts with their mega-event (or mega-league) partners, allowing for a true "smoothing" of their cash outlay?

We went back to recheck some numbers.

The English Premier League reportedly will increase sponsorship income by 50 percent during the next four years. And that position (for 2013–16) represents a 106 percent increase versus the four-year window of 2007–10. No "skyfall" over there.

Interestingly, the CSLS (as a representative sample of sponsors, properties and agencies) tells us annually that the vast majority of sponsorship spending is not on the mega-properties but on hundreds of national, regional and local properties. In fact, some 70 percent of sports sponsorship spending is on these types of smaller partners. And there, we believe, the rubber has left the road.

Properties are telling researchers that sponsorship works best when they are able to touch people, have potential customers experience their products and services and find platforms that relate to them in a meaningful (i.e., local) way.

So maybe the numbers don't lie . . . or haven't misled us at all. But the sports industry may do well to listen to what's going on out there. If you are a sports sponsorship seller, it may be time to hone your sponsorship sales strategies and take back market share from other non-sports properties.

We know sponsorship, in general, and sports sponsorship, specifically, work. We know it performs well in tight (or boom) economies. But at the moment, it is very possible sports are getting beaten off the bounce by other sector types.

Certainly, it's not our job, nor the job of this magazine or any single sports property, to wave the flag for sports sponsorships. But if we had our way, we'd ask who is keeping an eye on the weather charts or compiling the next decade's almanac.

From where we sit, sponsorship sector dominance for sports may be up for grabs in a few years, and if that day arrives the numbers won't lie. Rather, they will tell all.

6

Assessing the Impact of the NHL Lockout on Fans, Sponsors

Published February 18, 2013

NEARLY TWO MONTHS AGO, things looked bleak for the NHL. A second canceled season seemed inevitable, and the deliberate daily drip of damaging discussions degrading the game was disturbing. The players association talked about disbanding, and the legal maneuvering was debilitating. Everyone deserved a D.

Even Commissioner Gary Bettman's apology on Jan. 9 suggested the league understood it had once again harmed the game and there was unfortunate work to do.

"To the players who were very clear they wanted to be on the ice and not negotiating labor contracts, to our partners who support the league financially and personally, and most importantly to our fans, who love and have missed NHL hockey, I'm sorry," Bettman said. "I know that an explanation or an apology will not erase the hard feelings that have built up over the past few months, but I owe you an apology nevertheless."

It's February, and we'd like to know where things stand now. From a sports perspective, the NHL's players have come home, teams are fully staffed, and the compressed 48-game schedule is under way.

The season even started off with record TV ratings and sellouts across the board. Attention has moved from collective bargaining to expansion and the 2014 Olympic Games. So, everybody's good, right?

Not so fast. Modern sports business is largely about media and marketing, and the marketing reality of the NHL's new situation remains patently unclear. How is the NHL's marketing going? What would you do if you were the NHL's commissioner or CMO?

Do you think every NHL sponsor jumped back in with a full activation plan, or do you suspect some sponsors moved away from the NHL for 2013? If their contract didn't let them, are they considering not renewing once their contract is up? Have some of those newer fans from the NHL's recent growth years found alternative interests? Could the NHL's efforts fail to bring them back?

These questions fascinate us, and we know the answers aren't simple. We understand that collective-bargaining agreements and contracts are necessary realities in building strong partnerships between players and owners. We also know work stoppages can be cyclical in business and that, in the history of our industry, most stoppages led to better situations for both sides.

But professional sports does not even remotely resemble the factory worker or coal miner of the early 1900s or the retail service worker of 2013. Fans tend to be less sympathetic, particularly the second or third time around. History has shown fans are particularly disappointed when a champion is not awarded (see MLB 1994 and NHL 2005). Fortunately, this won't be the case for the NHL in 2013.

More importantly, we know people quickly discover they can do other things than watch hockey games . . . like working on company reports, downloading music or watching back episodes of *Breaking Bad* or *The Walking Dead* by way of iTunes or Netflix.

So we should ask the following:

• **Will we get a repeat of last year's NBA, when fans were thrilled by the high-intensity, shortened schedule?**

Many casual NBA fans can't even remember there was a lockout in 2011.

• **Will the NHL get that same forgiveness, or has the third lockout in two decades left a permanent mark?**

For the moment, it looks like forgiveness is still in vogue. NHL attendance is solid, and the media isn't taking pot shots at the NHL for having too many empty seats. In fact, ratings are hot.

• **What about the details of the deal? Is an eight- to 10-year deal long enough for sponsors to feel assured nothing will disrupt the game for another decade?**

Absolutely. Many marriages don't last that long, so getting a guarantee of eight years should be more than enough.

• **But what about the sponsors? Sponsors haven't said much on this topic perhaps because they couldn't hope to turn around in 10 days the way the teams and players did. Does that mean sponsors are still analyzing and pondering their future commitments this late into the season?**

We sense that the NHL has worked hard to keep these relationships solid and probably offered tasty make-goods for the damage done. And, logically, for many of these sponsors, this was not their first lockout/strike rodeo. Like the fans, we believe they're pleased to see a saved season.

"There's no question the NHL has to ramp up its efforts to appeal not only to its hard-core fan base but also to the casual ticket buyer or TV viewer," said Howard Dolgon, owner of the AHL Syracuse Crunch and a co-founder and former president of Alan Taylor Communications. "Activities over the past several months left a bad taste in the mouths of fans pertaining to both the NHL and the players. There were no winners in this battle, and the league, teams and players will need to put into place a long-term marketing/PR plan to clean up the damage caused by the lockout. It will take time and be no easy task, but I believe a unified effort from all interested parties will accomplish the goal over time."

As we roar through the first quarter of 2013, there remain numerous questions related to sponsorship. Which NHL players and clubs will best take advantage of the 48-game season for sponsorship/endorsement purposes? Which sponsorship sales strategies worked best to overcome CBA negativity? How will the NHL strategize to drive new sponsorship sales?

When the going gets tough, the tough skate extra shifts, work harder on their backhand and stay late after practice. We'd expect the same from all the champions in this league.

7

How Fan, Sponsor Reactions Factor into Team Decisions

Published December 10, 2012

HAVE YOU WONDERED if the Washington Nationals fully thought out their plan to bench star pitcher Stephen Strasburg in the midst of a tight National League pennant race in September? Are they looking back now and asking if their management decision needed to go beyond factoring in the health of a young right-hander's arm? Did they stop to consider their fans and sponsors?

Or how about when Tony Stewart caused a massive 25-car crash during NASCAR's October race at Talladega? Was he thinking about how his actions might bother his supporters and hurt his longtime sponsor, Office Depot?

Or perhaps you'd like to measure Red Bull's October backing of extreme parachutist Felix Baumgartner? Was Red Bull's marketing team at risk if this space-diving spectacular ended badly? Did they consider risk management and recovery marketing in their decisions?

We ask because maybe you've been involved in a similar situation where a key decision held the potential to alienate your fans or sponsors. Did you ask those hard questions and make informed, risk-based decisions? If you didn't, we'll throw some gas onto the glowing ember of your satisfied sponsorship thinking.

Social psychologists often talk about avid sports fan behavior in two distinct ways. The first holds that supporters of winning teams "bask in the reflected glory" of their team's most recent victory. It's called BIRGing and is best explained when fans tell each other, "We won!" all while making themselves unofficial members of the team.

The converse is called "cutting off reflected failure" (or CORFing) and is usually articulated as "They lost." In these instances, fans distance themselves from the team and place blame on the various parties who, in their mind, bungled the event's outcome. Both BIRGing and CORFing are widely accepted concepts.

So, one interesting aspect of Strasburg's summer saga was the very real issue of fan and sponsor reaction toward the Nationals for benching the team's best pitcher in the name of investment protection. If fans got mad, did they stay mad for long? Did it anger them even more when the Nationals lost Game 5 of the division playoffs to the St. Louis Cardinals? Worse still, were the Nationals' sponsors concerned about alienated fans enough to consider not renewing their sponsorships or reducing their future rights fees or activation spends?

We know the decision to remove Strasburg (15-6; 3.16 ERA, 159.3 innings pitched) was reportedly made by Nationals general manager Mike Rizzo and manager Davey Johnson and tied to total pitches thrown. It was supposedly worked out as early as spring training and designed to lengthen the career of a franchise-defining player who might lead this team for years to come.

On many athletic levels, it was logical. Who wants to wear responsibility for causing the elbow overuse that potentially destroyed a young man's career? But when Washington's season ended, some fans were probably looking for someone to blame. And while Nationals' management probably served as the first target, there is a distinct possibility some Washington sponsors caught subliminal heat as well.

How do we know that? Well, not so long ago, a pair of researchers from Northern Kentucky University investigated whether fans who were mad at a team might also blame the sponsors of the team. The genesis for that thinking comes from the balance theory (by psychologist Fritz Heider) that can be interpreted to suggest that if a fan loves a team and a sponsor supports that same franchise, the fan will feel good about the team's sponsors.

Is it possible, the NKU researchers asked, for the reverse to hold? Could fans, mad at the Nationals for benching Strasburg, take out their frustration on the brands they saw on the Nationals' scoreboard . . . big brands like Coca-Cola, Miller Lite and Geico? Possibly.

Even worse for the Nationals, could sponsors see the inflamed interest of the fans as a reason to reduce the priority of that sponsorship? Perhaps.

From a research standpoint, NKU's Vassilis Dalakas and Aron Levin looked solely at NASCAR fans and their identification with favorite drivers and their distinct dislike of opposing drivers. Fans of Dale Earnhardt Jr. were not going to cheer for Jeff Gordon or Stewart. Further, they were inclined to dislike sponsors of Gordon or Stewart simply for helping underwrite drivers they disliked.

Granted, NASCAR is not baseball, and dislike for a driver is certainly not the same as anger at a pro team's management. But hardcore fans react at every sporting event, and sponsors may want to rethink the real downside of fan anger. Team supporters may not hold a grudge long, but research suggests fan social identity and avidity can link up negatively with a team's sponsors.

In Korea, Sanghak Lee from Korea's Aerospace University is studying whether crashes are bad for NASCAR sponsors because the possibility exists that wrecks, while creating stronger brand recall, influence attitudes toward the brand, making the resultant brand association negative.

Many readers may doubt that, but at the very least some big league sponsors (or Stewart) should question the subliminal risks of in-season decisions and perhaps add logical responsibilities to their sponsorship contracts. If we can have dynamic ticket pricing for games, how far are we away from dynamic sponsorship contracts?

8

Are Ads Featuring Female Athletes Effective with Consumers?

Published October 15, 2012

MANY READERS may have noticed a large number of ads in August featuring female Olympians during and immediately following the London 2012 Summer Olympics. Kerri Walsh Jennings, Sanya Richards-Ross and Canadian Christine Sinclair seemed to be everywhere. And it was no surprise Gabby Douglas, after winning gold in gymnastics, suddenly smiled back at us from the front of Kellogg's Corn Flakes boxes.

It's certainly fitting female athletes were finally receiving more commercial endorsements, especially given American women won 58 medals, a number better than the overall medal tally for all but three countries (China, Russia, Great Britain) and more medals than the U.S. men.

But how many of those women will be able to cash in on their fame as endorsers, and how many will get featured in effective ads? Researchers John Antil and Matthew Robinson from the University of Delaware will soon publish data in the *Journal of Brand Strategy* suggesting American companies rarely employ female athletes as spokespeople, and when they do, many use them poorly.

We know from our own research and experiences that, with the exception of the superstars, most female Olympians and Paralympians do not "cash in" as many believe they should. Perhaps that shouldn't surprise us.

Historically, baseball players have promoted commercial brands since the late 1800s when tobacco brands first used celebrity cards to boost sales. In fact, Yankees slugger Babe Ruth got so popular they named a candy bar after him.

Still, the use of female athletes like tennis star Suzanne Lenglen or golfer Babe Didrikson lagged well behind their male counterparts, and it wasn't until 1933 that Didrikson got endorsements deals with Wheaties, Dodge cars and Wilson golf clubs.

Was that a function of male-controlled companies moving slowly to recognize the influence and buying power of women? In that pre–World War II era, advertisers often signed female entertainers for their glamour and lavish lifestyle, but female athletes were all but invisible.

The founder of the modern Olympic Games may have started that thinking. Baron Pierre de Coubertin didn't believe women should compete in the Olympics and prohibited their participation at the first Games in Athens in 1896. Even as late as 1912, de Coubertin was writing in the *Olympic Review*, "the Olympic Games should be reserved [only] for men. Can one grant women access to all Olympic competitions? No."

De Coubertin's anti-feminist stance was felt for decades and aspects of his sexism endured easily for another century. Remember, women weren't allowed to run the Olympic marathon until 1984 and can't start ski jumping until 2014. In fact, it wasn't until London 2012 that men and women participated in each of the athletic disciplines at the Summer Games.

Interestingly, Antil and Robinson's research found advertisers have long focused on a woman's youth, beauty or sex appeal at the expense of characteristics like courage, reliability and performance. Perhaps they feel only males can showcase those traits.

As an example, Antil points to a "Got Milk" ad from 2009 featuring a then 42-year-old Olympian Dara Torres in a bikini-style swimsuit. While Torres was obviously in world-class shape, it didn't impress many of the women surveyed.

"Female respondents said this was a poor image for an outstanding athlete who achieved so much while raising a daughter," Antil said. "Featuring Torres as a middle-aged single mother, able to balance family with work commitments, might have been more effective than highlighting her physical attractiveness in her 40s."

For many readers, the previous sentence represents a "gotcha" moment. It seems sexist however it's read, and particularly if the researchers (or columnists) relating this information are males. Torres was a swimmer. She had every right to pose in her swimsuit. That was her brand identity.

But during Antil and Robinson's focus groups, female participants watching ads featuring an attractive female athlete frequently provided negative responses. When an endorser was much younger than the consumer, the age difference made it challenging for female consumers to relate. In these instances, both the credibility of the young female athlete endorser and the product suffered with older female participants and didn't seem to move the needle with younger respondents.

Further, ads highlighting blatant sex appeal, such as ones featuring Danica Patrick in the shower for Go Daddy, seemed to produce heightened negative results especially when female consumers compared themselves to the spokeswoman. That's not surprising, but Go Daddy might not have cared. They were targeting men, and women's feelings toward Go Daddy probably didn't matter.

Research has long shown that many men relate strongly to male athletes like Michael Jordan or Michael Phelps, and male consumers aren't put off by appearance or achievement. Gatorade's legendary ad campaign "Be Like Mike" used song lyrics where men dreamed they were Jordan so they could fully emulate him.

Female consumers, however, appear to react differently to heroic endorsement by their own gender and may look less for recognition of heroic performances and more for an understanding of a shared struggle. Given that women are believed to purchase or influence 85 percent of all brand purchases, it's an interesting research question to ask why female endorsers aren't more visible. But if they are visible, should their use incorporate and feature the journey, not the destination?

In a year when more women than men participated on the U.S. Olympic team and won more gold medals (for the first time ever), one would think these women would enjoy increased endorsement opportunities. But perhaps this will only happen when advertisers better understand female customers.

Women may control the majority of household disposable spending and heavily influence household purchase decisions, but they appear to be very particular about who tells them what to buy and when to buy it.

9

How Can Sports Compete for the Hearts, Minds of Youth?

Published September 26, 2011

FORTY-FIVE YEARS AGO there were 70 teams playing in the big four professional sports leagues (NFL/AFL, MLB, NBA, and NHL). Today, with expansion and with the advent of MLS, that number has doubled. Add the myriad high-profile minor league, college and junior clubs, and the potential for clutter in the marketplace becomes much more obvious.

Take it a step further: Where once the average consumer experienced 2,000 messages per day via advertising and other communications like store signs, billboards or the sides of buses, today the average American sees or receives as many as 30,000 per day, even more for the hyper-engaged online. So we've doubled the number of teams and gone up by a factor of 15 on the number of communications, advertisements and audio-visual interruptions. Some simple math means we're at a 30x increment in possible distraction. And, don't forget the increasing number of mediums—online, offline, mobile, etc.

To that end, we've been wondering how the average child (if there is such a beast) actually becomes a fan of a sport, adopts a favorite club and develops team-aligned avidity . . . not to mention getting out and

2. A Syracuse home football game at its indoor arena, the Carrier Dome. *Courtesy of Syracuse University Athletics.*

playing that sport. For us, prolonged avidity is the lifeblood of pro sports, and this is where the proverbial rubber meets the road. When a fan is truly dedicated, game tickets and team merchandise are bought, sponsors buy signage at the stadium, advertisers buy spots on game broadcasts, and great athletes are drawn to play the game because the money is there.

But check this out: In addition to the cluttered environment, we're also dealing with a less active one. Do you think having played a sport creates some impact on fan avidity? We believe so, and other researchers have supported the notion that children are becoming less active. Recent stats showed that a mere 50 percent of 12- to 19-year-olds in North America actually participate in sports, a marked drop from a generation ago. The health implications notwithstanding, this is also a challenge for professional clubs.

But how are leagues and their member clubs accelerating that adoption process? How do they get kids more involved and interested and playing? As former hockey players, we're familiar with the NHL's efforts years ago to invest resources in street and roller hockey. That was a period when the NHL's marketing team (led then by Octagon's Rick Dudley) believed if they could place a stick in a young person's hands, they stood a chance of developing a new fan.

We're even familiar with a distant friend of ours who has been trying to shop a TV cartoon concept to the NHL called *Asphalt Avengers* in which various characters animatedly solve superhero problems in association with the NHL. We're not sure the NHL will option this concept, but it brings forth the question of whether any of the big leagues, in the midst of a staggering economy, lockouts, saturated airwaves, Facebook and various player misbehavior, can afford to spend much time thinking about five- to eight-year-olds or newly arrived immigrant children. At the very least, we know the big leagues—via their actions—have realized they need to communicate with youth in their language and via their chosen media . . . social, text and mobile. They get this, they're in this space, and more is undoubtedly coming.

We also know that parents play a huge role in what sport a child may adopt to play and/or follow and that sports greatly facilitates the concept of new-country assimilation. But in an age of single-parent families and significant brand clutter, it is worth wondering whether the biggest sports properties are fully investigating the consumer behavior pathways of their next generation of fans. We recommend they commit to that research now.

But it's not easy in an age of short-term profitability obligations to think about distribution channels, information overload and meaning transfer. Other industries interested in youth brand adoption have been doing it for decades, but the sports industry often shuns the specific market research long embraced by "traditional" consumer brands.

Let's not for a minute doubt that baby boomers are aging and will become less avid fans over time. We also know Generations X, Y and Z (the Net Generation) are smaller in aggregate and perhaps more fragmented due to media proliferation and increased consumption options. And, now we've got this aforementioned Internet Generation coming through . . . the kids of a small generation who are hyper-busy, multitasking online and often physically lazy. Screens are everywhere, the content options are sexy and attractive (not to mention non-sports-related), and those digital tablets are portable.

What's a sports marketer to do? Don't make the mistake of writing off clutter. There's no question the human brain is super-computer enough to disregard non-important brands and images. But what if your brand is increasingly lumped into that "delete" category? That's not good for your owners.

It's probably better to be proactive. If you are in charge of your brand's image or sustainability, you may want to make sure you understand modern children and early childhood cognition patterns. You may even want to conduct some research with children in your stadium (if you can find any) or at a sports facility where a future fan might already play your sport.

Kids say the darndest things, but they also hold the key to a lot of future revenue. We suggest you take them seriously.

10

As NFL Lockout Continues, Sponsors near the Death Zone

Published March 28, 2011

SOME OF YOU MAY REMEMBER a column we wrote a few months ago discussing the likely growth of sports sponsorship in North America during the next few years. That assumed, of course, that leagues like the NFL and NBA would avoid locking out players and moving their businesses from the sports pages and airwaves into the courtroom.

But that's the place where jurists' decisions might soon affect whether we see NFL touchdowns this September. It's a place of interest to anyone who studies the business of sport but not one where millions of fans want their favorite sports residing.

Now word comes out of Canada suggesting two sponsors are threatening a league with termination of sponsorship contracts if the league doesn't address a particular issue. That's right, Air Canada and Via Rail both have reportedly told the NHL they will withdraw their sponsorships (of clubs; neither is a league sponsor) if the league doesn't immediately get serious about those hits to the head that inevitably leave young men sprawled on the ice awaiting stretcher-bearers. A copy of Air Canada's letter to the NHL became public knowledge by social media just hours after it was sent.

You can understand NHL Commissioner Gary Bettman's dilemma. For most leagues, tradition is good, change is bad. For most sponsors, it's the league's traditions, entrenched images and valuable reputations that sponsors want linked to their brands. But Bettman now faces two sponsors demanding that hockey break with the most violent of its traditions and the accompanying danger of appearing to bow to sponsor demands.

Indeed, while fans may like hockey fights, even as they read that "enforcers" like Bob Probert might have died prematurely from taking too many fists to the face, the interest of a sponsor is quite different. Sponsors seek to sell their products and services via an association with a league/sport/team/player that provides idealized images that the sponsor's customers and potential customers might buy into.

For Bettman, the potential loss of one or two club sponsors can't be taken lightly. What if that thinking spread? What if some of the big-league sponsors considered using their leverage to protect their investments? Consider the recent Molson Coors sponsorship of the NHL. That's reportedly worth $475 million to a league where every dollar counts.

But let's set the NHL aside for a moment and ask the NFL about that same sponsor power. This is timely because starting March 11, NFL players decertified their union, the NFL locked out its players, and star players stepped forward to place their names on a lawsuit claiming the NFL had violated federal antitrust statutes. What happens to the corporate partners who invest $1 billion in fees with the NFL to achieve their own objectives via the league and what it represents? How will they respond?

One reality is that while fans hope the NFL won't miss games this September, time-conscious sponsors must stop production of TV, Internet, radio and print ads plus point-of-sale displays. Even product packaging bearing the NFL logo may need revising for marketing or contractual reasons.

Think about it. It's almost April, and the first game of the 2011 season is slated for the second week of September. That's five months away. Today, it's still possible to design, produce and ship those marketing materials. But fast-forward to May, when the CEOs of the big NFL sponsors realize their crack marketing teams have been hoping against hope the lockout would end and were only halfheartedly working on the alternative marketing tactics for the all-important last four months of the year.

How long before those CEOs pound their desks, call their marketing vice presidents and demand daily updates of whether the NFL has gotten its act together? Trust us, it's already happened.

In mountain climbing, there is always a turnaround point that you must honor. It can come from internal reasons (e.g., your health) or external forces (e.g., the weather). It requires that you stop going up and instead start getting down off the mountain immediately. This is particularly true in high-altitude situations where storms blow in unannounced and prolonged exposure in the "death zone" is what its name implies: deadly.

That metaphor is more appropriate than you might imagine for the NFL's partners as we head into April. Sponsor CEOs are forced to set turnaround dates for the NFL and look for alternate escape routes.

In other words, if the NFL isn't back to labor peace by May 1, these sponsor CEOs will force their teams to get off the mountain. They will take their hundreds of millions in spending and commit it to something else (if they can find suitable inventory). Perhaps sports but perhaps not. Arts? A cause? A festival?

One other thing may happen in light of the Air Canada and Via Rail announcements: Some NFL sponsor CEOs will likely call NFL Commissioner Roger Goodell and let him know their company does not look kindly on Goodell's team owners messing up the marketing plans of companies where one share point is worth billions in revenue and stock valuation. They may or may not let such communication go public.

Why? For CEOs at the tail end of a bad economy (and who are getting drilled by nervous chairs and volatile boards of directors), the loss of NFL games might cost them their jobs. NFL sponsorships work, and they differentiate key brands from their competition.

Losing that edge could make some brands mortal. It could make the CEO look ordinary.

To that end, maybe Air Canada is on to something. Maybe it's better to be proactive with your sponsorship dollars than passive. Maybe it's better to know when to get off the NFL mountain than risk that storm at 25,000 feet when you are exposed and vulnerable.

11

Understanding Why Sponsorship Continues to Grow

Published January 24, 2011

> They're like sleeping in a soft bed. Easy to get into and hard to get out of.
> —Hall of Fame catcher Johnny Bench, speaking on slumps

AS THE RECENT ECONOMIC FALLOUT settled in globally, but particularly in the United States, cutbacks in consumer and corporate spending were observed in numerous settings. And yet, despite the doubts and concerns of chairmen, CEOs and COOs, and despite bottom-line blame placed on numerous CFOs, researchers, marketers and sales staffs, sponsorship kept growing.

It's been an interesting conundrum (as Newman of TV's *Seinfeld* might say), because as 2011 begins and we watch CEOs (across the U.S. and Canada) increasingly announce improved quarterly results, the marketing budgets of most organizations appear radically different from five years ago. Just look at the reductions in hospitality budgets or companywide moratoriums on travel to corporate-sponsored events.

This has meant that, like crazed, wild-haired scientists, we've been obligated to ask, "Why is it so?"

The two most-read analyses of sponsorship spending in North America—IEG's *Sponsorship Report* and the Canadian Sponsorship Landscape Study—both noted that although there was reduced growth rate in companies' investment in sponsorship, it continued to grow (or, at least not contract to any great extent) in 2009 and is expected to grow again in 2010 in the U.S., Canada and globally.

Likewise, the PricewaterhouseCoopers' hospitality and leisure sector report for 2010–13 suggested that sponsorship would remain the fastest-growing global sports sector, eclipsing gate revenue, media rights and merchandising by a compounded annual growth rate (CAGR) of 4.6 percent.

All of these studies are supported by happenings in the marketplace. The IOC last year announced two new first-time TOP sponsors (Dow Chemical and Procter & Gamble) to its stable of partners, now at 11, who commit an estimated nine figures each quadrennium for the rights to associate with the Olympic Games. Rumors abound that a 12th TOP sponsor will be added in 2011.

In Russia alone, MegaFon ($260 million), Rostelecom ($260 million), Aeroflot ($180 million), Rosneft ($180 million) and Volkswagen ($100 million) are readying five-year plans to inject nearly $1 billion into the Sochi 2014 Olympic Games. This outpouring of financial support from national partners continues the trend established for the Vancouver 2010 Games, where a reported $750 million was contributed by Canadian sponsors.

How, we ask, is this possible and why is it happening?

First, sponsorship works. There are dozens of academic studies and hundreds of professionally produced evaluations backing this up. Sponsorship is an effective tool to reposition brands, alter consumer perceptions and increase sales. In fact, one of our Ph.D. dissertations found more than 150 objectives that marketers had established as reasons to invest in and embark upon a sponsorship.

Second, sponsorship works efficiently. By this, we mean research has shown the effectiveness of sponsorship to reach specific target markets through association with properties that resonate with those markets. Think Burton Snowboards, Shaun White and snowboarders, or Gillette, baseball and men who shave.

Third, sponsorship works better than advertising. Although debate still exists over the difference between advertising and sponsorship, there is general agreement among many that the two marketing tools are notably different and play different roles.

These three theories support the argument that it is the association differentiating sponsorship from advertising. The old saw has been that advertising is one-dimensional and non-personal, whereas consumers who follow sponsorships see the sponsor, the sports property and the linked association between them.

Quite simply, as the consumer is exposed to the association, images are more easily transferred from sponsor to property and vice versa. Conversely, in a (typical) nonintegrated advertisement, the consumer sees the advertisement (often shown during a sports event or on a sports website) but without a compelling association to the property. Each has its advantages and disadvantages, but most will agree that sponsorship is a hybrid form of advertising.

Fourth, sponsorship appears to be more fun, with hospitality, backstage passes and locker room visits; plus it can be staged to incorporate a social responsibility hook to aggressively assuage the guilt that accompanies massive investments in activities that appear (to some) socially trivial. In other words, sponsorship can benefit a charity while executives tour the pits or drop the ceremonial first puck.

But all is not perfect in the sponsorship world, and PwC notes that the mercurial economy "has focused a rising proportion of attention and spending on the biggest sports brands with global reach and pulling-power." This means "mid-level brands [properties] have found it harder to attract major sponsors while sponsorship of the smaller local sports brands has been hit [hard] by potential backers reducing discretionary spend in the economic downturn."

To be sure, it is notable that sponsorship continues to grow and in North America will reach a CAGR of 5 percent in 2012 and 5.6 percent in 2013. The question for many is whether the biggest fish

(NFL, IOC, FIFA, EPL, UEFA, etc.) will leave the minnows high and dry.

We'll also have to watch to see if player strikes, owner lockouts or terrorism change sponsorship's trajectory.

12

Could Sponsor Alliance Spread to North American Sports?

Published September 27, 2010

WE RECENTLY READ with great interest the following news brief out of Europe. Since many North American sports practitioners don't follow Formula One closely, we thought it worthwhile to re-present the sponsorship tidbit in its full form:

F1 Sponsors Form Alliance

LONDON: The top 100 Formula One racing sponsors have formed an organization aimed at adding their voice to the direction of the sport. Dubbed the F100, the alliance comprises individuals and sponsors that support the teams including Diageo, Puma, LG, SAP, Shell, and Vodafone. The aim of the group is to provide sponsors with the opportunity to shape the future of the sport and maximize their investment. Formula One commercial rights boss, Bernie Ecclestone, will review the proceedings, with the first of three proposed annual meetings taking place in London on 1 September.

Did it make you wonder what might happen if sponsors of the NFL, NASCAR or NHL suddenly grabbed power in a bloodless coup? What if sponsors from all major North American sports were to form a syndicate? Could the minnows (even though some of them spend in excess of $50 million a year on sponsorship) redirect the whales?

What about the possible benefits for the sponsors and for sponsorship in general? In the case of the F100, they invest a reported $705 million in the sponsorship of F1 annually and believe that an alliance will enhance their benefits. Are they right? Could formalization actually lead to improved sponsorship activation and evaluation?

First, we have to ask if the thought of sponsor collusion or strategic alliance (depending on your point of view) in the North American context is even remotely possible.

Your first reaction might acknowledge that most sports leagues and teams draw the majority of their revenue from broadcast rights packages and ticket sales. Sponsorship to these rights holders is critical, but many treat sponsors as something to be endured:

We'll take your money . . . thank you very much . . . but don't get too pushy. Remember, we are the rights holder. You (the sponsor) only have cash, perhaps a bit of useful product and some advertising to offer.

But lately, certain sports leagues and teams have pushed their overhead costs to the limit, rendering the revenue from sponsorship necessary. When a team loses a key sponsor, it can mean the difference between profitability and running a loss. In turn, the resulting decreases in available payroll could change a contending, playoff-bound club into an also-ran. This dichotomy is important to examine. The team, league, sanctioning body or event frequently considers sponsorship to be a messy third-tier revenue stream, but when the money isn't there, the house of cards starts to wobble.

So what would happen if North American sponsors bound themselves together and brought their collective muscle to bear on every single property? What if they demanded ratings data similar to what we find via advertising? What if sponsors told leagues, No more drugs? What if partners told sponsees that they wanted to be treated differently? What if they demanded evaluations of sponsorship effectiveness based on conservative and reliable metrics? What if they had claw-back clauses based on athlete, coach and team off-the-field behavior? Where could this go?

Much of this discussion depends on your perspective. Are sponsors trying to take power or merely asking for greater opportunities to be heard (and to be recognized for their increasingly important status in the sports business)? More importantly, will leagues feel threatened by this behavior or welcome it?

"The time has come for the sponsors to share peer knowledge, index various properties and get their say on how sponsorship should be run," says Paul Pednault, director of the recently formed International Guild of Sponsors. "Sponsorship directors have come a long way, from sales promotions considerations to integrated brand activations. Many now have degrees in marketing, research and sports management. Some are lawyers or have Ph.Ds. It's logical that sponsoring corporations will eventually share their knowledge and experience to promote the health, the growth and the craft of sponsorship worldwide."

Industry analyses support what Pednault is saying and further emphasize why sponsors have the option to take a stand where they didn't as little as a decade ago. The two best-known North American studies of the sponsorship landscape, IEG Sponsorship Report and the Canadian Sponsorship Landscape Study, have repeatedly reported increases in the expenditures on sponsorship, even during the recent recession. These annual studies also report sponsorship's increasing importance in the marketing mix of corporations and the increased sophistication (i.e., use of agencies, evaluation and activation) in its use.

So what does this all mean for the sports business? What has the F100 started? Has it awakened sponsors to the inevitable, that the need to form alliances for the better good of sponsors, and arguably sponsorship, is upon us?

This F100 concept is not particularly new, and sponsors of the Olympics (companies like Coca-Cola, Visa and McDonald's) have met privately in the past to point out their sponsorship concerns to the International Olympic Committee. While their objective was not to stage a revolution, they knew the economies of scale they controlled were significant.

But North American sports properties and rights holders should not be surprised if this groundswell continues and sponsors start to shift the paradigm. From where we sit, sponsorship is meant to offer an equally weighted partnership, where the benefit scales are balanced. Perhaps our European cousins believe this is not the case, or perhaps they are the first to respond to sponsorship's increasing importance in sport business. Stay tuned.

13

When Athletes Become Legends, Do Their Sponsors Also?

Published August 2, 2010

AT 2:58 P.M. local Vancouver time on Feb. 28, Sidney Crosby went from superstar to legendary icon status as more than 65 percent of his fellow countrymen (and women) watched him score a thrilling overtime goal to help Canada win Olympic hockey gold at the 2010 Olympic Games.

A win for Crosby, a win for Canada, a win for the Vancouver Olympic Games, a win for the International Olympic Committee . . . but was it a win for those IOC sponsors that spent small fortunes associating with the Games and, de facto, the athletes? And, what about Crosby's long-standing sponsors, the ones that have been with him for years and have built marketing programs around him?

Does an epic performance for an already established charismatic superstar elevate him to the level of some of the personalities like Michael Jordan, Arnold Palmer and the others noted in the table?

The *Hockey News* recently reported that Crosby was on the verge of signing a five- to seven-year, $10 million deal with Reebok, which the article reported would be the richest endorsement deal in NHL history. With the addition of Reebok, it would give Crosby, who has already won a Stanley Cup with Pittsburgh, a stable of loyal sponsors including blue-chip brands such as Tim Hortons, Gatorade and Bell.

To explore this concept, we reached out to our friends at Gatorade Canada to learn more about the concept of instant-icon status for a player and whether the ensuing euphoria spreads to the sponsor as well. Like any good evaluation, we needed to start from a benchmark. Gatorade has been with Crosby since it signed him as a 17-year-old in 2005. Pre-Olympics internal market research by Gatorade in Canada told us:

1. Between 2007 and 2009, consumer tracking studies found almost one-third of Canadian respondents purchased Gatorade product with a particular Crosby/NHL promotion. So, at some level, the Crosby sponsorship was already driving purchase intent in some demographic segments

2. A December 2009 omnibus of 1,000 interviews with Canadians over the age of 15 regarding corporate spokespersons found that Crosby had exceptional awareness scores across Canada:

    a. 78 percent awareness

    b. 85 percent popularity, with 53 percent at very popular (top 3 on a scale of 10)

    c. 79 percent believe Crosby an "excellent fit" with Gatorade

    d. Nearly 1 in 5 Canadians (17 percent) able (unaided) to name Gatorade as a Crosby sponsor

    e. Gatorade was the second-strongest linked sponsor to Crosby (after Tim Hortons) and strongest linkage to "G" of all six spokespersons in the study.

So people know Crosby, he's very popular, and a large segment of the population knows well that Gatorade sponsors him. But is the Crosby–Gatorade association now known to more than 17 percent of Canadians? Has it moved to where one-third of the population knows of the association, toward the levels achieved by only the greatest of athlete sponsorships (think Michael Jordan and Nike in the U.S.)?

"Gatorade is and always will be about being associated with top athletes and helping them take their game to the next level," said Dale

Table 1. Memorable Athlete–Sponsor Associations

Athlete	Sponsor(s)
Lance Armstrong	Nike, U.S. Postal Service
Dale Earnhardt Sr.	GM Goodwrench, Wrangler
Derek Jeter	Gillette, Gatorade, Ford
Michael Jordan	Nike, Gatorade, McDonald's, Hanes
Peyton Manning	MasterCard, DirecTV, Sprint, ESPN
Arnold Palmer	Pennzoil, John Deere
Richard Petty	STP
Maria Sharapova	Nike
Venus Williams	Reebok
Tiger Woods	Nike, Gillette

Hooper, head of marketing for Gatorade in Canada. "We definitely feel our association with Sidney is stronger after Feb. 28 than it was before, given his legendary status in Canada. Other athletes realize that Gatorade fuels Sidney, and can fuel them to successes also."

Andy Harkness, an executive at SDI Marketing, who has worked on the Gatorade file and with Crosby for many years, said, "Sidney's performance at the Olympics had the ability to take Gatorade somewhere where the Gatorade brand couldn't go by itself and, in turn, has validated Gatorade as the sports authority through the brand's link to Sidney. We've leveraged this to build excitement with Gatorade's customers and our sales teams already."

So, do the sponsors become legends as well? It's not yet scientific but it would appear the right sponsor proactively positioned with the right athlete can certainly sell more product while driving higher awareness, positive public relations and untold YouTube hits for their brand.

Legendary? Maybe. Profitable? Most certainly. The trick it would appear (perhaps as it has always been) is to identify the athletes before they are world-beaters and have your marketing campaign geared up for the moment they put it all together.

Brands and marketers also must recognize that working with celebrities has its risks. If an athlete gets arrested or revealed in a tawdry or salacious scandal, brands have to be prepared to withstand the public relations heat or implement an exit strategy.

14

Strategy Session: Keys to Marketing to Youth

Published November 23, 2009

MARKETING TO YOUTH? Ha, that's up there with herding cats, stabbing mercury, bottling lightning and managing the Cubs into the World Series. Not impossible but certainly a challenge.

One key to youth marketing (12–17) is bringing an unfailing honesty in the brand's message and keeping a thick skin when the early results aren't perfect. That's because most 12- to 17-year-olds are rapidly entering a phase of their lives they neither fully understand nor completely control.

The 12s are still children who are rapidly attempting to emulate the nearest 17s. The 14 and 15s are simply confused and generally dealing with hormones, pimples and parents who, as Will Smith once sang, just don't understand. And the 17s are trying to act like college kids. It's a quagmire. So when speaking to this mangy group, the common approach seems to be to grab something that is fashionably relevant and try to make it work. "Get me Hannah Montana." "Bring me the next Jonas Brothers." "Does anyone know a skateboarder?"

I would suggest avoiding that route and going with something authentic and true to the brand's heritage, new product development

3. Syracuse basketball fans get fired up for a home game against Duke. *Courtesy of Syracuse University Athletics.*

or existing positioning platform. That's because by the time the brand's strategy is formulated, the budget is revised, the creative is tweaked and the superstar director or studio photographer hired, the trend has shifted . . . ever so slightly. The kids have zigged (or zagged), and many marketers are left fumbling.

But take heart. As The Who told us, "the kids are all right." They will work with you if you tell them the truth, avoid clichés and let them stay up late playing *Madden* or Facebooking their faces off.

PART TWO

The Olympics

15

IOC Has Opportunity to Create True International Sports Network

Published October 26, 2015

IN THE 1980S, the International Olympic Committee and its marketing vice president of the time, Dick Pound, changed the way our industry looked at big sponsorships. That happened with the creation of the TOP program for sponsors that provided high-value exclusivity for brands like Visa, McDonald's, and Coca-Cola to reach billions of consumers in hundreds of nations.

In late October, following a round of public interviews, we found ourselves wondering if the IOC had done it again. Had the global team based in Lausanne, Switzerland, come up with a logical (yet revolutionary) idea to use IOC muscle to leverage its global scope? It certainly seemed that way when IOC President Thomas Bach told Universal Sports Network's viewers the launch of an Olympic television channel (whether by linear TV or Internet) was rapidly moving forward. Bach even went as far as to confirm he expected a free digital Olympic Channel to launch sometime in 2016. That would seem to be historically bold.

Here's what we mean. When Bill Rasmussen conceived the idea of a national sports network with ESPN in 1979, most industry experts laughed. Sports on TV could never make enough economic sense to support a 24/7 programming platform. But it did, and ESPN was a relatively quick success.

Not surprisingly, many of the same people who thought such a national sports network was preposterous strongly challenged the 24/7 regional sports network concept. That was until superstations like WGN, YES Network, and TBS made it work. Years later, there are RSNs in almost every market in the country with more than 500,000 homes.

Meanwhile, at the national level, ESPN has long since been joined by Fox Sports 1, NBC Sports Network and sport- or league-specific networks such as the NFL Network, NBA TV, Big Ten Network, and Golf Channel.

We won't debate the health of the national and regional sports networks, but we think the IOC's move to create an international sports network with national and regional tentacles is notable. Many readers may suggest ESPN already operates internationally, but we'd argue most ESPN- or Rupert Murdoch–owned networks are nationally and/or regionally focused. What makes the IOC's move interesting is the idea of a singular programming source (based in Madrid) for a worldwide audience.

From both a business and content management perspective, the move is risky. We're all different, have different cultural interests and speak different tongues. But the IOC's risk is potentially mitigated since sport is a universal (if not common) language. Given the capacity for viewers to select the audio band they wish to use (i.e., English, French, Spanish, German, Russian, Italian, Chinese, Japanese, Korean, Swahili, etc.), it is not hard imagining most humans will find a language where they can decipher the words and match them up with the video.

In June, the IOC announced the plan to launch its own Olympic television channel as part of Bach's Agenda 2020 plan. The target date for the new network was April 2016 or just prior to the 2016 Rio de Janeiro Summer Olympic Games. Most assumed the Olympic Channel debut would come in the form of an over-the-top digital package, thus avoiding terrestrial, cable or satellite system operators controlling distribution. By October, however, the IOC was hinting that traditional distribution could happen quickly.

Interestingly, U.S. Olympic Committee chairman Larry Probst has been leading the Olympic Channel Commission, whose high-profile membership holds responsibility for delivering content on each of the 35 Olympic sports. A recent press release suggested that the IOC's investment will cover more than $500 million over the first seven years of the network, including the build-out of a digital platform to support the phone and tablet universe.

So here's today's pop quiz question: Can an international network work as a stand-alone business today? Or, framed another way, while global viewers may like Olympic-themed content, is the business model sustainable?

"The decision to proceed at this time was taken after consultation with the IOC's broadcast partners," Pound said recently. "The broadcasters believe an Olympic channel will assist in maintaining an interest in the Games between broadcasts of the Games themselves."

There's nothing wrong with the IOC wanting to goose its ratings during their every-other-year mega-events. For many in our sports universe, if a property is not on TV, it doesn't exist. That's not good for the IOC.

But there's another key reason for the IOC to push forward: keeping the international sport federations of the Olympic world happy.

"IFs hope to gain broader exposure for their own events," Pound said. "While the current plan is to launch the Olympic Channel prior to the Rio Games, the main objective is ensuring the project is firmly established before it is rolled out."

Satisfying international federations is one thing. But the IOC also needs to keep the national Olympic committees on board and, de facto, their various national governing bodies. The move to an international channel, if it isn't dominated by any one country (or continent), will serve valuable vested-interest purposes.

"The Olympic channel will serve the important function of promoting Olympic sport in the periods between Games," said USOC

Chief Executive Officer Scott Blackmun. "It can also be used to help attract a younger audience for Olympic sport programming, which is critically important to the future of the Olympic Movement."

Last thought: If you felt ESPN was an industry game-changer in 1979, you'll want to watch how quickly the IOC's concept catches on with FIFA, UEFA, the NBA, or UFC. Sports with true global followings will have no choice but to replicate this international network platform for themselves.

16

How Will Olympic Sponsors Respond to Future Host Sites?

Published March 10, 2014

THE SOCHI OLYMPICS have ended . . . and thankfully, they concluded safely. The XXII Olympic Winter Games were highlighted by a record number of qualified countries (88), heartbreaking losses by the American men's and women's hockey teams, and the emergence of skier Mikaela Shiffrin, who probably slalomed right into Lindsey Vonn's endorsement vacuum. By all accounts, the athletes were treated with great respect and enjoyed their Russian experiences.

But what about the off-the-field marketing battles, the ones involving sponsors and their swarming sports marketing agencies? Who won those slugfests? Were Coke's "controversial" ads a reason to proclaim them the advertising winner? Did longtime TOP sponsor Visa gain market share with its inspiring, athlete-focused promotional strategy? Or, did P&G's "Thank you, Mom" campaign carry the day? P&G's 39 YouTube videos certainly seemed to win the online Olympics, given the millions who watched the branded content via social networks.

And what did we learn about location? Many were deeply concerned pre-Games about the athletes, the TV ratings, human rights and terrorism. However, as noted, these concerns were not realized. In fact, in most cases, the opposite was true, and given the ever-increasing number of online viewers, NBC must be pleased with television ratings up slightly from 2006, the last European-based Games.

But perhaps even more importantly: How important is location to sponsors of the International Olympic Committee?

Recent studies led by a colleague of ours, John Nadeau, have shown the importance of the host country's image to sponsorship due to the vast reach and following of the Olympic Games. Image transfer is a well-researched aspect of sponsorship and one that many scholars believe differentiates that specific platform from advertising and other promotional strategies. Conceptually, it refers to sponsorship's vibrant capacity to associate the images of a property to a sponsor, thereby alternating the perceived images of the sponsor in the minds of targeted consumers. Nadeau's work (of which O'Reilly is a co-author) finds that the images of the host country also enter into the minds of these consumers.

Practically, beneficial image transfer is understood by sponsors and is generally the reason they align with sports, leagues, teams and players. Now, in the cases of mega-events and national teams, as Nadeau's results support, country becomes an important source of alignment. Brands want a net positive association or rub-off that will add value and drive recognition and sales. But negative transfer is rarely studied, and in Sochi there was much concern about what was really going on.

Example: Some Sochi sponsors were reportedly forced to develop sympathy advertising in case a horrific terrorist attack took place. Further, numerous sponsors likely developed "go black" plans to ensure their advertising was not linked to terrorism if that story broke. These backup plans are not completely unusual (in and of themselves), but they interest us because of the location of the 2014 Winter Olympics and the host countries of a number of future Games.

For now, the IOC's global sponsors, TOP partners like McDonald's, Visa, GE, P&G, Dow and Coca-Cola, are fully invested in the Games and other associated properties, including the Youth Olympic Games. In fact, the IOC's outgoing marketing chief, Gerhard Heiberg, had hoped to bring the TOP sponsorship portfolio up from 10 to 12 but ran into the very real issue of the Russian anti-gay propaganda law during his key selling window. As it was, Heiberg said a number of sponsors around the world, but particularly TOP sponsors, were concerned about Russia's position on human-rights issues. Location again affects sponsorship.

On the sponsorship front, sophistication has grown so much and permeates far below global levels now. National programs, national sport organizations, state and provincial sport organizations, qualifying events, national championships, athletes—and on and on the list goes of properties or assets related to country or nation.

One thing we learned is that the host country matters and matters a lot. Sochi, Rio (2016) and Pyeongchang (2018) are not dream locations for North American marketers. Tokyo in 2020 looks good, but the list of candidates for 2022 has some options that would be less attractive to a North American marketer, such as Krakow (Poland), Almaty (Kazakhstan) and Lviv (Ukraine)—although a return to Oslo (Norway) or Beijing has some marketing upside. The upcoming FIFA World Cup in Qatar (2022) probably holds similar concerns for global sponsors.

What does this really mean? It suggests that if the IOC takes the Olympics to the wrong places, it can create distressing marketing outcomes (albeit positive societal ones), and the logical first responders to issues like questionable site selections will be the sponsors. They must receive positive image transfer, or they won't re-sign with sports properties that damage their brands or fail to draw sufficient eyeballs to justify massive investments.

17

Bach's History a Signal That His Leadership Will Be Proactive

Published February 10, 2014

THE SOCHI OLYMPICS have started, and the world is holding its collective breath. Will these Games come off safely?

We'll know for certain in the next fortnight, but the guy we bet can hold his breath longest is new International Olympic Committee President Thomas Bach. These are his inaugural Games, so it's the first time he has stood in front of billions to open an Olympiad. He's a global visionary, but we're guessing you still don't know much about this lawyer, businessman, politician and competitor.

In a word, he is fiercely competitive. We know this because he won gold at the 1976 Montreal Olympic Games for West Germany in the team foil competition. He's also a two-time world champion, which means he likes a good individual duel. Just ask the U.S. Olympic Committee. It learned the hard way in its negotiations over broadcast revenue as it related to U.S. bids to host the Summer Games. The USOC sent New York (2005) and Chicago (2009) out to fight, and both were sent home quickly.

So have no doubt Bach came to Sochi ready for Russian President Vladimir Putin's Ring of Steel (as it relates to terrorism) just as much as he arrived ready to deal with any slight associated with gay rights.

"Fear is a very bad adviser," Bach told the media recently. "It is not a category in which I think."

What does Bach's presidency mean for sports in North America? Will the results mirror those of former Olympic sailor Jacques Rogge, whose 12-year IOC term was characterized by organizational stability, increased revenue, heightened focus on anti-doping and the launch of the Youth Olympic Games, but also a pronounced fatigue at the end of his presidency? Our guess is no.

In all likelihood, sports history will remember Rogge as an effective manager who followed the tumultuous reign of Juan Antonio Samaranch with a cool hand on the tiller. Bach won't seek the same approach to consistency and stability. Instead, we think he'll attack the big issues that concern him.

Bach knows the IOC's quirks and politics, having served as a board member since 1996, earning roles as vice president from 2000 to 2004 and from 2006 to 2013. Before 1996, he served as a member of multiple IOC commissions. He also was a supervisory board member for Germany's FIFA World Cup in 2006.

According to the IOC's Dick Pound, the former head of the World Anti-Doping Agency and longtime vice president of the IOC's marketing efforts, "Bach will bring a whole new level of energy to the IOC and Olympic movement and ultimately try to energize the IOC into something more than a rubber-stamp process for approval of executive board decisions. There are many new issues and challenges he will face, and I expect until Sochi is behind him, he'll spend his time assessing the nature of the team he wants to put together."

Here's where we think Bach's foil is pointed:

The Soviet gay propaganda law appropriately received major attention in North America, where gay rights are important and influential. And while IOC monitoring of Russia's human-rights initiatives was expected, Bach placed some very public pressure on Russia's Putin at the end of January, when he made clear Olympians could champion equality and inclusion in press conferences, but the Olympic charter ban on making political statements during competition or medal ceremonies would stand. Given Germany's open culture toward homosexuality, we expect Bach will privately support athlete anger associated with this issue. For Bach, inclusion will not be a cliché.

More efficient bidding. Bach led the second-place Munich 2018 bid and was quoted as saying he wants to reduce process costs and time. Given the two recent failed U.S. bids and the significant costs incurred, this may help more U.S. cities to consider hosting future Games . . . but only if the USOC and IOC have truly patched up their differences over broadcast revenue sharing.

Bach just finished presiding over his first initial bid process—for the 2022 Winter Olympics—and knows Oslo, Norway; Beijing/Zhangjiakou, China; Almaty, Kazakhstan; Krakow, Poland/Jasna, Slovakia; and Lviv, Ukraine, want to host the world. Interestingly, voters in Stockholm (January 2014) and Munich (November 2013) rejected bidding, citing projected costs. This must have stung Bach, since he is from Wurzburg, north of Munich, and knew Stockholm, which hosted the 1912 Summer Games, would have become the first city to ever host both the Summer and Winter Games. How Sochi unfolds will influence Bach's management of 2022's winner.

Bach's engagement of the USOC should matter to league commissioners Adam Silver (NBA), Gary Bettman (NHL), Don Garber (MLS), Laurel Richie (WNBA) and Bud Selig's MLB replacement (projected for early 2015) because the U.S. has not hosted the Olympics since 2002 and won't before 2024 at the earliest. Stated simply, basketball, hockey, soccer and baseball are part of the international sports landscape and influenced by their respective international federations relative to competition, drug testing and seasonality. If North American leagues wish to expand overseas or showcase their athletes in global competition on U.S. soil in 2024 or 2026, they will have to play ball with Bach and the international federations.

American sports practitioners may not yet care about the new IOC president, but we think they soon will. Bach's coronation and ascendency continues a trend of growing European clout when it comes to charting the growth and global visibility of America's domestic sports leagues.

And Bach will not fear the USOC or its big leagues. He'll come right at them.

18

What Is Your Sports Property Doing to Build, Keep Its Fan Base?

Published July 22, 2013

WE KNOW that many sports business professionals haven't been too concerned to learn Russian President Vladimir Putin and others are well on their way to spending $60 billion to stage the February 2014 Winter Olympics and Paralympics in Sochi. If the Russians want to set the all-time host-city spending record on behalf of the International Olympic Committee, who among us should really care?

Certainly, other host cities could have spent much more (Beijing's $42 billion in 2008 comes to mind, although many believe the Chinese actually spent far more) and London 2012 probably could have "pounded it," but it was appropriately restrained and reportedly stayed under $20 billion.

So when we size up Sochi's spending, we're forced to admit the Russians have not been shy . . . even if much of the investment has come from politically prodded private-sector money. It matters not. What was once a rural town near the Georgian border is well on its way to becoming a world-class beach/ski resort that will draw tourists and outdoor enthusiasts for generations to come.

But is this the right approach for the IOC and the Olympics? Should the staggering amounts spent by the host city-state matter?

Will future regions simply cozy up to governmental or private industry underwriters to fill out this trend? It depends on someone's true (or secret) agenda.

For $80 billion, Alaskan oil money could develop a ski hill and resort destination near Mount McKinley. Or maybe Newfoundland Hydro could do something with the World Heritage Site Gros Morne and turn an environmental jewel into a tourist destination. Think what the Australian mining companies could do with the Great Barrier Reef or Ayers Rock.

It's not an easy question, particularly when pesky taxpayer dollars are concerned. Still, as usual, we have more than a few comments.

First, will the topic of Olympic gigantism influence Rio 2016 and Pyeongchang 2018? Does $60 billion in Russia mean we're not far removed from the first $100 billion Games? And, while the IOC has put some controls on Games size—capping the number of athletes and sports and encouraging temporary facilities—the desire to put on the best show might float future budgets where one-upping the previous host city matters.

Secondly, and this is a little darker although far from rare, what are the geopolitical ramifications when a country uses the Olympics to make a statement about its wealth, politics or policies? Diplomatic columnists frequently suggested that Beijing 2008 was a "coming-out" party for China's communist government and burgeoning economy. In short, one of the objectives of the 2008 Games was to show the world that China was truly a first-world country.

Well, mission accomplished. Others have done similar things, including St. Louis 1904, Berlin 1936, Tokyo 1964, Montreal 1976, Moscow 1984 and Sydney 2000. In the case of Berlin 1936, let's not forget that what lay behind that big investment was the staging of the Games as a platform for German nationalism and a springboard for Adolf Hitler to war. Those efforts ultimately crippled the world for the next nine years (if not more) and forced the cancellation of the Olympics through 1948.

With respect to the U.S., in both 1984 and 1996, American planners made commercial statements in their staging of the Los Angeles and Atlanta Games. But where Los Angeles was praised for its distinctive (and creative) private financing, Atlanta was panned for its engagement of crass investors such as sponsors, merchandisers and licensees.

In retrospect, many in the Olympic movement begrudgingly acknowledged the U.S. helped push the IOC toward a fiscal orientation of profitability and sustainability. Canadian Dick Pound, as longtime IOC vice president of marketing, further modernized IOC strategies and helped steer the Olympic movement toward greater revenue performances.

And thirdly, let's not forget tourism—key driver of recent megaevent investments—which has become one of the sought-after impacts of any Games. Sydney, Vancouver, Turin, Beijing and, now, Sochi all focused on this key output throughout the prospecting, bidding and Games-winning phases. We know from our own academic research that Olympic Games do change country images in the minds of international tourists. They work, and Beijing 2008 absolutely changed how Americans and Canadians view China.

So what to make of Sochi's expensive Games? There are a few points of view. Financial investment aside, we see Sochi 2014 as a skilled blending of the third point, tourism, with a solid mix of the political. If we're right, one might say the Russians are building a brilliant disguise. Yes, brilliant.

Russia will put its beaches, mountains, rugged beauty and ability to build a world-class resort in a few years on display. And not only will it host the Winter Olympics, but it also will be getting the Formula One Russian Grand Prix and key games during the 2018 FIFA World Cup.

All of that will help the Russians move their image from the old, lingering perceptions of Cold War, vodka, KHL hockey and female tennis players to that of an industrious country capable of high-level work in a spectacular sea-to-sky world. But is there more to it than meets the eye?

Hard to say. But if you have $80 billion lying around, know that you can do the same for your favorite town.

19

Soaring Cost of Olympic Host Bids Concerns Ueberroth

Published August 20, 2012

AS THE HIGHLY SUCCESSFUL LONDON OLYMPICS came to a close, there were probably very few senior sport leaders thinking about calling Peter Ueberroth. They were probably anxious to get out of London and start focusing their energies on the ramp-ups for Sochi, Russia, in 2014 and Rio de Janeiro in 2016.

But we'd advise those same titans of Olympic sport, be they International Olympic Committee administrators, sport ministers or sport CEOs, to think about arranging a short meeting with the former U.S. Olympic Committee board chairman to get his thoughts on how the Olympics have changed and will further morph in the future.

We made that call to the chief organizer of the 1984 Los Angeles Summer Olympics—the privately held, profit-generating Games that served as the turning point for the Olympics as a business. Ueberroth, 74, is one of the few Olympic architects who can look back on the past and comment, with clarity, on the "best practices" of past Games.

"Basically, when we received the Games for '84, the people of Los Angeles had voted not to spend a single penny on the Olympics," Ueberroth said. "So we studied all the previous Games, and it took us about 30 minutes to see that only 1948 in London made sense for how we could think about going forward. Remember, the Brits were on food rationing then and rebuilding their city less than a decade after getting bombed in the early '40s. But they staged '48 in a manner that worked."

For Ueberroth, that cost sensitivity is important in discussing how the Olympic movement must move forward in the 21st century. Interestingly, though, the former commissioner of Major League Baseball didn't linger long on how staging costs had "grown by a factor of 10 to 20 times." Similarly, his voice was not filled with concern when he noted that host-city spending and Games gigantism were out of control or that some recent cities have "left legacies of costly and unused facilities that, in some cases, left a negative effect on troubled economies."

It was something more than past inefficiency that concerned him.

"I think the immediate trend, going forward, is that fewer countries will be bidding in the next three to four cycles. We're already seeing that for 2020, where the IOC is only allowing three cities [Istanbul, Madrid and Tokyo] to proceed toward the final vote [Sept. 7, 2013, in Buenos Aires, Argentina]. I wouldn't be surprised to see more cities dropping out in the future, thus keeping the IOC from having the robust list of candidate cities that we've seen in the past."

How does the IOC resolve that?

"I really hope the IOC can encourage future bid cities by making the requirements much simpler, by requiring less expenditure, and that the actual bid process is not so expensive," continued Ueberroth, who remembers a time when Los Angeles was the only city in the world willing to take on the job of hosting the Olympics. "It doesn't serve anybody in the present world economy to have these Games costing the amounts they do."

Numerous reports suggest that Chicago spent close to $80 million on its unsuccessful bid for the 2016 Games. If that trend continues, some IOC experts believe that only countries, not cities, will be able to afford the up-front bidding costs plus the full financial guarantee the IOC requires to stage the Olympics. Even in a moderately stronger economy, most American cities would have to think hard about whether they could convince taxpayers to go out on a limb for the Olympics, particularly when they know there will be no federal bailout.

Still, Ueberroth believes that an environment where Olympic bids will have many applicants can be continued.

"There was extremely positive change in the 2012 Games," said Ueberroth, who visited London during the first few days of the Games. "Virtually everything there has a solid after-life and is very beneficial to the neighborhoods and country. It's been a positive reversal to the three Games that preceded London. Sir Sebastian Coe has won another gold medal, to go with the one he won in L.A. in 1984 in the 1,500, with his leadership of the 2012 Games."

Does Ueberroth think the U.S. could host the Games again, especially after the recent announcement the IOC and USOC had reached a new revenue-sharing agreement for the next 20 years?

"Larry Probst [current USOC chairman] has accomplished the difficult task of reframing a new financial relationship that appears to be fair to both the IOC and the U.S.," Ueberroth said. "Things were at a place where the USOC administration during my term failed. It was a personal failure, not the people with me, to find an economic long-term agreement. What Larry has done removes one of the obstacles for a U.S. bid. There are other obstacles, but a carefully well-thought-out bid has a chance."

If that's right, perhaps Ueberroth's Los Angeles legacy, in which Games were staged in 29 cities, nine counties and three U.S. states, might come back into play, and his counsel, rich with real history, would be again sought on how the IOC ensures more cities bidding, better use of funds and a more sustainable Olympic movement.

20

Beyond London: Building on Olympic Fan, Sponsor Interest

Published July 30, 2012

AS THE LONDON 2012 GAMES get under way, the thoughts of most fans are likely on the athletes and the competition. However, many working in sports were already thinking beyond London.

We know staffs at Olympic committees around the world are revising their plans for Sochi 2014 and Rio 2016 for both existing elite athletes and for the development of new Olympians.

In Canada, Christopher Overholt, CEO and secretary-general of the Canadian Olympic Committee, has a number of things on his plate. First, he is dealing with the post-Olympic reality that accompanied Vancouver's hosting of the 2010 Winter Games. Second, he has to ensure Canada continues to perform in the medal count like it did in British Columbia. And finally, but not solely, Overholt must play a role in determining whether Canada should bid again to host the Olympics either in Toronto (summer) or Quebec City (winter).

Overholt, whose career in professional sports has included senior positions with the Miami Dolphins, Florida Panthers and Toronto Raptors, began his work with the COC about a year ago. We asked him about the challenge of leading a national organization at such a crossroads.

"When we all arrived here together, I saw it as a very unique opportunity, where Vancouver was the platform from which we could build a new and different architecture for Canada's Olympic future that perhaps didn't exist before," Overholt said. "We could focus our attention on our athletes and their stories due to the heightened profile they'd built in Vancouver. Most importantly, though, we wanted to construct a platform that brought attention to our Olympic athletes 365 days a year, not just in the immediate vicinity of the Games."

Among the COC's first moves was to adopt a professional sports view of the world. Although some in the Canadian press believed this was too slick for Olympic sports, Overholt's core executive team did not.

"Our focus needed to be different," he said. "We immediately began to focus on how we are known to Canadians, the emotional connection they have with the COC. We did research and observed, learning that this emotional connection was through the athletes. Our brand is the Canadian Olympic team, and the heart of our brand is the athletes. But following the Vancouver Games, we started to look at this new brand, and we moved to a Canadian team [trade]mark that was a mosaic of our athletes. This was a tactical decision to change how we portrayed ourselves to Canadians, to consumers and to our partners."

We asked what specific tactics were undertaken to implement this shift.

"We looked at the connection points to people through the Games and looked for ways to remove the times between Games where we have little or no impact," he said. "We do this in two ways. First, with help from partners, you have to identify platforms that your partners can attach to. Based on our research, we started to focus on things like innovation and the 'higher, stronger, faster' motto. We also started to talk about health and wellness and how sport and Olympics can aid that. We also focused on aspects of sustainability. Vancouver set the standard for a carbon-neutral Games, which we knew was important to consumers and, more importantly, to our athletes."

The COC's recently launched "Give Your Everything" campaign focuses specifically on athletes.

"Second," Overholt said, "we looked at our event schedule. I drew on my experience with the NFL, which used to be about just the schedule and the Super Bowl, but now they've built it out to include ongoing interest and properties like the spring combine and the draft. We followed this model and are seeking to build our own platforms outside of the Games."

The key, as Overholt's previous experiences have shown, is to fill the calendar and make the COC a platform that holds constant interest.

The current marketing and branding efforts are built around the athletes and provide knowledge about them by telling their stories. Overholt describes the effort as "showing Canadians what it means to be an Olympian" by communicating the time, effort and support needed be athlete. He also described the implementation strategy, which includes a filmmaker, video and social media experts, a vastly enhanced interactive website and direct athlete involvement. He spoke of the COC's desire to maintain a professional sport acumen and build strength and relevance. Is it working?

Overholt pointed to an aggressive promotion at a subway station in Toronto that recently generated 8 million impressions, at a rate of 1 million per week. The COC's Hall of Fame Gala in 2011 raised $2.1 million, and, in the past year, its YouTube viewership has gone from less than 2,000 to more than 130,000. The current athlete-based marketing campaign has generated a 96 percent increase in Web traffic, nearly 300 million impressions, a Twitter reach of more than 11 million and nearly 200,000 Facebook likes.

Overholt was quiet on the COC's future plans on Olympic bids, but he did note Canada's solid reputation in the Olympic movement to deliver great Games. Our view is that the COC would be mistaken to not bid aggressively on future Summer and Winter Games given this reputation, his strategy, and the obvious benefits that have resulted.

Overholt would say his work is far from finished. Regardless of Canada's performance in London and the outcome of Olympic host bidding, his squad is determined to change the dynamic of the "every four years" mentality.

21

Deighton Balances Economic Realities with Legacy Expectations

Published June 18, 2012

IF YOU WERE OFFERED the opportunity to serve as CEO for a Summer Olympic Games and could choose any six-year period in the past century to fund-raise for those Games, it's quite possible 2006–12 would sit squarely at the bottom of your list. Maybe then and during the Great Depression of 1929–35.

Unfortunately for London 2012 CEO Paul Deighton, that luxury of choice wasn't available. London won the right to host the '12 Olympic Games in July 2005, and less than a year later, Deighton made the decision to leave his post as Goldman Sachs' European COO to tackle Europe's third Olympiad in eight years (following Athens in 2004 and Turin in 2006).

Flash forward six years. London's Games start next month, and while the North American economy is gaining traction, the past half-decade has been characterized by a global recession with many European countries and businesses hit hard.

Despite these conditions, London (with the 2012 Games, the Queen's Diamond Jubilee and the English Premier League) might be Europe's shining star. In fact, a July 2011 research study by Visa

Europe suggested London should see an extra $3.3 billion worth of economic activity from the Games, drawn from direct consumer spending, associated activities meeting demands created by that spending and increased residential income.

Still, a few financial and legacy concerns, most notably a skyrocketing security tab of more than $1.5 billion, have been steadily arising in advance of the opening ceremony on July 27.

"Taking into account costs outside the package, the full cost to the public of the Games and legacy projects is already heading for around £11 billion [$17 billion]," said Margaret Hodge, chair of Britain's Public Accounts Committee, in March. "The venues and infrastructure of the London Olympic Games are on track to be delivered on time and within budget. However, the £9.3 billion [$14.4 billion] public-sector funding package is close to being used up, and we're concerned whether the running of the Games will be held within budget."

For Deighton, pre-Games announcements by government officials showing the Games are, for the moment, financially under control is gratifying. But constant hinting that doom awaits or security spending is out of control probably weighs heavily on his mind.

"We are exactly where we want to be," Deighton said while praising his team's ability to raise almost $3 billion in sponsorships. "We're in a great place. That's not to say there haven't been challenges along the way and not to say there isn't much still to be done."

Deighton emphasized it was not just corporate support that was holding up, but ticket buying as well. Revenue in that space has exceeded expectations on most fronts, and with less than 45 days to go, tickets for 25 of the 26 sports had sold out in the first wave of ticket sales (although new release ticket purchases this month have reportedly been sluggish). Further, merchandise guarantees have been in place with more than 50 licensees since just after the Games were awarded.

On the labor front, the London Organizing Committee for the Olympic Games has more than 6,000 employees on staff and more than 70,000 volunteers getting ready, all 76,000 of them presumably pumping revenue into London's various pubs and shops. Even better, Deighton suggested all of the Olympic Park venues and other new infrastructure investments have been delivered on time, meeting all requirements for a successful Olympic and Paralympic Games.

That's impressive, but what about the legacies the London bidders promised the International Olympic Committee when they won the right to host the Games? Could a sluggish economy and tighter government budgets curtail the Games' final legacy?

In a February report by the House of Commons reviewing preparations to date, numerous elements related to the Games and the British government's management of taxpayer investments were raised. With an investment from government approaching $17 billion for legacies and the facilities promised, projecting overages (which the government guaranteed to cover) already feels like a full-contact sport.

Most obvious target? Security costs are skyrocketing and seemingly costing new millions each day. In light of London's 2011 riots, Deighton has been forced to address not only international terrorism but also domestic order. "There are a number of different threats that you get with any event of this scale and prominence," he said. "Our plan is very comprehensive, very detailed and has components, for example, that were already very focused on any potential public-order threats—though, consistent with any security plan, you're focused on making it risk-based."

Parliament's report also makes clear that only 109,000 British citizens are new regular sport participants, well below the original goal of 1 million new sport participants (by March 2013)—this despite a nearly $700 million investment in participation legacy via the national governing bodies.

It also discusses issues related to legacy (e.g., socio-economic regeneration of East London) and notes clearly, "this rings alarm bells about the effective integration of the various legacy plans and about clear accountability to us [Parliament] and the taxpayer. When we return to the examination of the Olympic legacy, we expect clarity over precisely who will be accountable to Parliament for delivering the benefits to taxpayers from their significant spending on this program."

When we asked Deighton about this concept of legacy, he noted the most important driver was to have staged a great Olympiad. In his mind, delivering great Games becomes the catalyst for opportunity. He also emphasized non-sport legacies, like new skills gained, and sustainable jobs in particular are already emerging with strong results. In addition, the plan, which includes breaking even financially, is to keep facility construction to a minimum while maximizing temporary facilities.

Deighton already knows London's sporting legacy will take longer to ascertain, and U.K. residents may bring their traditional skepticism to bear. But at a time when many nearby countries are struggling, London 2012 should deliver one of the most basic Olympian quests: hope for a brighter tomorrow.

22

How IOC's Pound Sees Anti-doping, Marketing Efforts Evolving

Published April 23, 2012

THERE'S NO QUESTION that Dick Pound, a swimmer on the Canadian Olympic team (Rome 1960) and longtime International Olympic Committee member, has played a significant role in designing the commercial underpinning of the IOC. And since Pound's efforts have included the creation of The Olympic Program and management of the World Anti-Doping Agency, we went to Pound, one of the IOC's most outspoken members, to ask for his thoughts on TOP and WADA on the eve of London's historic 2012 Summer Olympics.

It was soon after Montreal's 1976 Games that Pound was elected president of the Canadian Olympic Committee, followed in 1978 by full IOC membership. He was later selected chairman of the IOC's Marketing Commission and installed as the founding president of WADA.

From 1999 to 2007, Pound not only led WADA administratively but was its face and voice, engaging in memorable debates with America's professional sports leagues, elite cyclists and uncooperative international federations. Under his leadership, significant progress was made in the fight against doping, although many in sports hated Pound for his dogged pursuit of each entity's dirtiest chemical secrets.

While the IOC was no doubt thankful he was placing anti-doping on the world's front pages, Pound bore the brunt of league attacks, athlete stonewalling and player–union deflection.

So where are we in 2012?

"WADA's active role remains the same," said Pound. "We've got to monitor, fight, improve our labs, identify shortcomings and give credit where it's deserved. But we're not there yet. What WADA risks losing as it becomes more established are the excitement and willingness to confront organized cheating."

It's notable Pound uses the words "excitement" and "willingness to confront," but it's his zeal that separates Pound from his peers and has made him an Olympic outlier . . . a man for his seasons.

WADA faces a changing environment in which public perceptions and awareness are "decent" but drug-story fatigue is making it harder to keep WADA on the world's front pages. How to change that? Pound provocatively suggests the active involvement and engagement of Olympic sponsors and sports event sponsors, parties that support sports and are adversely affected by a culture of doping.

He also thinks the decreasing number of positive doping tests is creating an illusion. He bases that on the facts that "there have been cutbacks on the number of tests, many testing protocols are still poorly structured and that 'cheaters' remain ahead of the testers in many aspects."

While we might lack true insight about testing protocols or cheaters, as parents and industry veterans, we can comfortably ask: Who do you want watching your flock at night . . . a committed person or a comfortable person? The same holds with marketing. After 30 years of TOP, do you stick with something comfortable or commit yourself to the warts-and-all review?

The TOP concept was first unveiled in 1983, by Horst Dassler of Adidas. Shortly thereafter, IOC President Juan Antonio Samaranch tapped Pound to drive a worldwide sponsorship agenda and create a protocol where global sponsorship rights were efficiently bundled. The IOC's objective was to make the concept operational by the 1988 Games in Calgary and Seoul. When it started, TOP generated less

4. A snowboarder passes through the Olympic rings at the Vancouver Games. *Courtesy of Andrew Burton.*

than $100 million for the first quadrennial cycle. By 2012, TOP was generating more than $1 billion. Today, TOP provides 11 sponsors with exclusive Olympic brand rights in all jurisdictions where the IOC acknowledges national Olympic committees.

But is TOP still doing a good job? Or is the Olympic brand possibly losing some of its relevance for sponsors seeking to connect with young consumers?

"Well, I certainly think some of the events we've added are giving back value and attracting youth," Pound said, discussing specific Olympic events like snowboarding, mountain biking and freestyle skiing. "And, it's not impossible to conclude that after all the effort of bringing younger people into contact with the Olympic Games, we've expanded the Olympic brand. TOP's roster illuminates that."

Can a nearly 30-year-old concept, still dominated by American sponsors (six of the 11), hold up?

"Because TOP is an international program and because we've been careful about picking companies that are really international in scope, we're in a position to generate benefits globally for them in almost all economic circumstances. This works because, if things are, say, bad in the U.S. economically, they may be going well in other parts of the world and vice versa. That has been one of the key success factors of TOP. It's almost like it's a way of balancing it out economically. It's a form of financial hedging."

Asked whether TOP would get overhauled in the future, Pound replied, "The choice of attractive and exclusive categories, allowing our partners to use global strategies, with flexibility in particular markets for shaping their specific messages, is key. Whether TOP will change, well, frankly, we put everything on the table about three or four years ago, to review the many alternatives and considered whether we should have a completely new paradigm or maintain what we have now. Upon review, we realized we actually have a pretty good formula and have benefited from all the attributes I just mentioned. So we opted not to change merely for the sake of change."

Nonetheless, change is coming, and it will start with the portion of the TOP agreement that gives the U.S. Olympic Committee roughly 20 percent of most TOP deals. That the USOC could secure that agreement in the 1980s speaks to the importance of U.S.-based sponsors buying into a global concept and the USOC knowing foreign sponsors would want to reach into U.S. pocketbooks. But with many IOC members openly acknowledging the Olympics will not return to the U.S. until TOP and U.S. broadcast rights revenue is redrawn (and redistributed), TOP is likely to get a face-lift.

Will that happen before the London 2012 Games? Probably not. But Pound, an architect of so many Olympian platforms, thinks London will offer enormous opportunities to countries, sponsors and athletes alike to shine on the world stage. And somewhere behind the scenes he'll be working on agendas that push the Olympic movement forward.

23

Analysis Must Show NHL the Value of Olympic Competition

Published May 3, 2010

ONE OF US recently had the good fortune to be the guest of the Anaheim Ducks when they hosted the Vancouver Canucks at an entertaining, late-season, playoff-style game on a Southern California Friday night. The home team won in storybook fashion following a dramatic shootout.

The "Olympic Effect"—as we like to call it—was on full display. More than 2,000 Vancouver fans were on hand sporting Canucks jerseys but also Team Canada jerseys and flags. The 15,000 (or so) Ducks fans were decked out as well, although a number of them were visible in the Team Canada Scott Niedermayer jerseys. Numerous other Team USA and Team Canada jerseys were evident. The two national anthems were played to thunderous cheers, and a prominent display featured the Olympic jerseys of each Ducks' Olympian. At times, it was hard to decipher between "GO DUCKS GO" and "GO CANUCKS GO."

The atmosphere was electric.

Would this game have been as powerful if there'd been no Olympics this past winter? We ask because the jury is still out on the NHL's

5. Anaheim Ducks Olympians representing their club and country. *Courtesy of Debora Robinson/NHLI via Getty Images.*

participation in the 2014 Games in Sochi, Russia, but there's no doubt its 2010 participation created a significant benefit for the league and its stakeholders. The gold-medal game between Canada and the U.S. in particular delivered a massive lift. NBC sportscaster Bob Costas called it "one of the greatest sports events I have ever seen," and NHL Commissioner Gary Bettman summarized it as "a great experience for hockey . . . [because] from a North American standpoint, more people watched hockey than ever before."

The TV ratings numbers in the U.S. and Canada speak volumes (courtesy of Nielsen). In the U.S.:

• It was the second-most successful Winter Olympics ever (190 million viewers), trailing only the 1994 Lillehammer Games, when the Tonya Harding–Nancy Kerrigan scandal attracted curious eyeballs near and far.

• During the 17-day period of the Games, the Olympics on NBC attracted 9 percent more viewers than their three rivals combined (Fox/CBS/ABC).

• The Canada—USA final was the most-watched hockey game in 30 years (since the gold-medal game versus Finland at the 1980 Olympics following the "Miracle on Ice" semifinal victory, which attracted an audience of 34.2 million on tape delay) with an average viewership of 27.6 million and a peak audience of 34.8 million during the final hour of the game (from 5:30 to 6 p.m.). That's 10.5 million viewers more than watched the 2002 gold-medal game, also between Canada and the U.S., at the Salt Lake Games.

In Canada, the Vancouver Games were the most popular event in the country's history, with more than half of Canada's 33 million people (16.6 million) watching the gold-medal game and more than a third tuning in for the opening and closing ceremonies. Of particular note: The top five events from Vancouver were also the top five most-watched television programs in Canadian history. All shows, all genres. Ever.

Those numbers are all terrific, but what was the lasting impact? Did the NHL and NHL Players' Association activate on this opportunity like they should have? Were they ready to leverage this success a month later?

Some might argue that while the Olympics helped the sport, they might not have served the best interests of the NHL. Some, including Washington Capitals owner Ted Leonsis, have suggested "investors" are not getting a fair exchange of value back for the risk they take in sending their assets (players) to the Games. Other owners note imbalances between the revenue their players help generate for the Olympics and their actual (or hard) return in taking that related risk.

That thinking isn't greedy or overtly capitalistic as much as logical for anyone working in the entertainment industry.

On the player side, the view is different. As was obvious to anyone who attended or watched the Olympics on TV or the Internet, the NHL's players want to be there and want to win medals. Some players, including stars such as Alex Ovechkin, have even said they will play in 2014 regardless of what the NHL says.

Wait. Say that again. A player like Ovechkin might "walk off the job" to play in the Olympics? Imagine the fines, outrage and disruption. Imagine the increased visibility, personal brand-building and financial upside.

We doubt it will come to that, but between now and 2014 it would be nice for sports economists (academic or otherwise) to articulate a value for Bettman on what the Olympics are worth to each entity (International Olympic Committee, host city, NHL, NHLPA, individual players). How much did the NHL benefit in dollars? How much did they leave on the table? What was the brand lift for the tabulators of good will as well as the wallets of players like Sidney Crosby and Ryan Miller?

Conversely, if the NHL doesn't go to Sochi in 2014 but the Russian-financed Kontinental Hockey League does, what will the KHL gain during a home-ice tournament? What will the NHL lose? Could Sochi provide the stimulus for a long-whispered merger concept between two leagues on different continents that ultimately creates a hockey super league?

Financial analysis, some of it probably already in the works, will undoubtedly reveal all. Given the global (and digital) economies that now prevail and the consumption revolution taking place through revenue-generating properties like the iTunes store, we think hockey fans, flexing their economies of scale, will dictate the solution.

24

U.N. Role Offers IOC Chance to Place Sport amid Global Priorities

Published April 5, 2010

LIKE US, a few of you may have read with mild interest the October 2009 press announcement that the United Nations had granted the International Olympic Committee official observer status.

And like us, you may have been a bit perplexed and thought, "How could this only be happening in 2009?" Both organizations are venerable, established and, most would agree, far-reaching. The U.N., founded in 1945 after World War II, has 192 member nations, while the IOC, founded in 1894, has 205 member national Olympic committees, representing 205 jurisdictions globally.

Given that more countries marched in the Beijing Summer Olympic Games than are recognized by the U.N., all waving their flags proudly, some of you probably thought the IOC was just a better political machine. So why is this even worth talking about?

We think it is for two reasons. First, this announcement was another demonstration of sport's continued influence in larger society, but also it might point out sport's past failure to strategically link to higher global priorities such as health, education, equality (including racial, gender and religious), environmental concerns, the fight against AIDS and world peace.

But make no mistake: No one person, company or organization controls sport, and considerable progress in addressing social causes has been made in the last 50 years. In that sense, only a contrarian might bark that sport has not done enough for underserved communities. The issue, as always, is doing more.

Secondly, and this ties to the first point, this official U.N. role provides a tremendous platform for the IOC to lead so many sports (Olympic or not) in addressing social issues.

But hang on.

Does U.N. observer status even matter? By most accounts, U.N. observers hold little true power and influence. Generally speaking, U.N. observer status is a distinct privilege that should give the IOC the ability to participate in U.N. activities and the right to speak at U.N. General Assembly meetings (but not vote on resolutions).

But what if observer status provides the IOC, the champion of the Olympic movement and arguably the most powerful sport organization in the world, a seat at the most important global political table in the world? That seat might then provide IOC, its stakeholders, and its members with opportunities to involve sport in global priorities and to communicate as much to its vast membership.

IOC President Jacques Rogge was quoted in the original press release as saying, "This is a huge recognition of the role sport can play in contributing to a better and more peaceful world. The Olympic values clearly match the U.N.'s philosophy. Today's decision further strengthens the partnership between the IOC and the U.N. system."

All well and good, and the IOC president is nothing if not diplomatic. But coming off the 19-month high of Beijing 2008 and Vancouver 2010, we can now ask a series of tougher questions for the various bodies involved with this landmark anointment:

• Has the IOC quietly become the world's best nonpolitical vehicle (a sport-bearing Trojan horse, if you will) to broker social change or influence those governments most likely to pull up their drawbridges at the first sign of a U.N. peacekeeper?

• If the IOC is in fact that vehicle, do its members, always elected on their commitment to sport and the values of fair competition, hold a larger obligation than selecting sports to be played, rules for sports and cities for sports to be played in? To wit, should IOC members in the future be selected with a strategic eye toward peace, prosperity and pollution?

• Should the U.N. think strongly about the IOC playing a more significant role in guiding the future of the planet? After all, the IOC can assemble more countries for a parade than the U.N. Plus, the IOC can get the networks of the world to cover their quadrennial proceedings (and pay for the privilege to boot).

• Should future global sponsors of the IOC and upcoming Games in London 2012, Sochi 2014 and Rio 2016 enter into these agreements (or uphold them) with a stronger commitment to the IOC and its many Olympism in Action causes (environment, women, education, peace)? Should IOC sponsors, as part of their global corporate social responsibility agenda, take to heart the IOC's U.N. observer status? Said another way, should IOC sponsors be advised that by aligning with the Olympics, they are expected to save the world?

We're not sure of the specific answers. The operational concepts of the U.N. and IOC, particularly after the completion of a spectacular Winter Games, seem awfully vague relative to quarterly reports, the world economy, job security and world peace.

But as two Olympic fans looking into the crystal ball from up here in the ivory tower, we see gray uncertainty—call it clouds of apathy—out there with only a hint of golden outcome. This might be one of those issues more of us in the Olympic family should continue investigating. That, or we need more contrarians pushing us to reach beyond the mediocre.

25

Opportunity Now for Paralympics to Grab N. American Spotlight

Published March 15, 2010

SO HERE'S A QUESTION FOR YOU . . . how come no one really seems to care about the Paralympics even though they are amazingly great? And we mean that sincerely. Why doesn't anyone, or more than a few select folks, really talk these Games up?

Because, truly, the Vancouver 2010 Paralympics, which began Friday and run through next Sunday, will feature some of the greatest sports performances of this decade-old millennium, and yet we fear very little coverage will seep out of the frigid North and make waves on our respective wire services, blogs, Internets and Twitters. Certainly, the 2008 Paralympics in Beijing, with 100,000 strong crowds at the Bird's Nest, were special. But that was most likely a blip, and we could find ourselves back to sparse crowds of family, friends and a few true spectators in Vancouver and Whistler. Why is that?

At the risk of sounding like Dana Carvey's infamous *Saturday Night Live* Church Lady . . . could it be money? Ratings? An absence of athletic stereotypes? Or is it Satan?

What about the fact that sports around the world are trying to better promote links to health and be socially responsible? Is this not an ideal vehicle and platform to do that? Isn't it possible that an athlete who uses a wheelchair represents at least one epitome of working to overcome the evils of obesity (even when unable to stand unassisted)?

"This is definitely the 'coming out' for Paralympic Sport in Canada and the USA, and will bring us up to speed with the leaders in Paralympic coverage and support—U.K., Australia, Germany, France, Brazil, Korea where consumer awareness is much higher and there has long been historical TV coverage," said Anna Parisi, chief of communications for the Canadian Paralympic Committee. "The challenge for Canada and the USA is to use this opportunity to create a nation of fans and to sustain interest when the Paralympic Games isn't quite so close to home."

Imagine that: Six hundred athletes, from 45 countries, all of them overcoming tremendous physical odds, competing for 64 gold medals in 20 events spread over 10 days in five sports (alpine skiing, cross-country skiing, wheelchair curling, ice sled hockey and biathlon), and we are only now in North America, in 2010, getting to the tipping point that other countries reached long ago. How is it possible that America and Canada, two bastions of sports, actually trail in this debate?

"The Vancouver Paralympic Games are bringing energy and awareness to our movement," said Charlie Huebner, chief of Paralympics for the USOC. "It is allowing the U.S. Olympic Committee to significantly enhance Paralympic programming available to kids with physical disabilities and injured service members at the community level throughout the United States."

Huebner's counterpart at the Canadian Paralympic Committee feels the same way and has worked to ensure that CTV's Olympic broadcast consortium will feature more than 50 hours of television programming of the Paralympics, including plans to show the sled hockey gold-medal game live. This is by far the most TV coverage ever for the Paralympics in Canada.

"Operating in the shadow of the Olympics, while a challenge, may also end up being a blessing given the commercialism around the Olympics and Olympians compared to the more family friendly and warmth of the Paralympic Games," said Henry Storgaard, the CPC's chief executive officer. "So I agree that this is a unique opportunity to shine a light on North American Paralympians."

As professors at Syracuse, we don't need that spotlight to shine very far. Goose Perez (East Syracuse), Jim Pierce (North Syracuse) and James "Jimmy Jam" Joseph (New Hartford) give us local heroes. Those three made the U.S. wheelchair curling team. And then we have three more players from the Buffalo area in Brad Emmerson (Amherst, N.Y.), Mike Blabac (Buffalo) and Alexi Salamone (Grand Island, N.Y.) to cheer for in sled hockey.

One other thing. Make no mistake in thinking these are Johnny-come-lately Paralympics. Vancouver represents the 10th Paralympic Winter Games, and it's the second time Canada will have hosted Paralympians (Toronto held the 1976 Summer Paralympics). Given that Salt Lake hosted the Paralympic Games in 2002 and Atlanta the 1996 Summer Paralympics, we all should be substantially aware of disability sport. But are we?

We argue that we're actually where many organizations are when they move from introduction to growth in their life cycle. This may sound overly academic, but it is true. We have a product with tremendous potential and a track record. We have a market that should be supportive but likely is not fully aware of what our product offers. We have limited direct competition but many substitutes exist. So, what is the strategy?

Simple really: establish your distinction (done!), build awareness of it (starting) and generate resources (key). In some countries, the resources come from the government. In others, it arrives via a blend of sponsorship, private giving and national Olympic committee commitment.

Whatever the source, the U.S. and Canada sports communities should see the Vancouver Paralympic Games as a place to fully press the inclusivity buttons that motivate greater awareness, athlete identification, coaching and marketing/communications leverage of our collective (and amazing) Paralympians.

26

U.S. Facing a Generation without Playing Host to Olympics

Published November 9, 2009

AS YOU MIGHT HAVE NOTICED, coverage of future Olympic Games in some U.S. newspapers declined significantly after Oct. 2, when International Olympic Committee voters in Copenhagen, Denmark, humbled Chicago by eliminating the Windy City in the first round of the 2016 bidding.

There are a number of potential reasons for this drop-off in stories, ranging from subliminal anger over Chicago's dismissal to the realities of a busy North American fall calendar where the NFL, MLB, NBA, NHL, MLS and NCAA are fully engaged.

But what if it was something else? Could it be a subtle editorial realization that the Olympics may not visit North America again for more than a decade? Is it possible we've just witnessed the end of an Olympic Golden Age when North American cities hosted the Olympic Games on average once every 5.55 years? Think about it.

There were nine Olympics on our continent in the last 50 years (1960–2010). At the moment, the earliest we could see the next Games is 2020, but probably 2022. Neither the U.S. Olympic Committee nor the Canadian Olympic Committee bid for Winter 2018, and it has been suggested the U.S. won't bid for 2020.

Conclusion? The earliest North America might see the Games is if Toronto (2020) or perhaps Quebec City or Denver (2022) bid and win. That is virtually a generational age. It means an American child born in 2002 will be at least twenty years old before seeing an Olympic Games hosted in the U.S. again.

It made us wonder what that might mean for Olympic sport avidity and for U.S.-based sponsors of the Olympic movement such as Coca-Cola, Visa, McDonald's and General Electric. Does it portend a possible drop-off in corporate financial support? Could it possibly push some of the smaller nonrevenue sports to the brink of virtual discontinuation?

One of North America's most important Olympic figures, IOC member Dick Pound, picked up on that theme during his recent visit to our campus. "I think it could affect domestic sponsorship if the Games are not held in North America for an extended period of time," he told students. "The billion-dollars-plus in Olympic and domestic sponsorship the IOC has generated for the next quadrennial is critical to the health of national Olympic committees and sport development worldwide."

Pound's insights are further illuminated when one considers the IOC is actively pursuing younger generations with projects like the inaugural Youth Olympic Games (for 14- to 18-year-olds) Aug. 14–26, 2010, in Singapore. With more modern X Games–type sports seemingly invented every day (not to mention graphic video games), are young North American archers suddenly at risk?

The answer could be yes, and not just for smaller sports. At the Singapore YOG, water polo, synchronized swimming, slalom canoe and road and track cycling won't be contested.

Clearly, hosting the Olympics is good for sports business and good for the development or sustenance of a sport, and a review of past modern Olympic Games shows how often the Games have hit North America in their history. Not surprisingly, of the 12 times listed, the U.S. hosted the vast majority (eight). To illustrate, we collected the following data and arranged it by decade.

It's clear that the "rate of hosting" for the 30-year period of 1990–2019 has declined to 20 percent from the previous 30-year average

Table 2. Tracking North America as Olympic Host

Decade	Games	N.A. Games	% in N.A.	Sites
1890s	1	0	0%	
1900s	4	1	25%	St. Louis
1910s	1	0	0%	
1920s	5	0	0%	
1930s	4	2	50%	Lake Placid, N.Y.; Los Angeles
1940s	2	0	0%	
1950s	4	0	0%	
1960s	6	2	33%	Squaw Valley, Calif.; Mexico City
1970s	4	1	25%	Montreal
1980s	6	3	50%	Lake Placid, N.Y.; Los Angeles; Calgary
1990s	5	1	20%	Atlanta
2000s	5	1	20%	Salt Lake City
2010s	5	1	20%	Vancouver

Source: www.olympic.org.

(1960–89), when 37.5 percent of Olympic Games were held in North America. And, if our forecasts are accurate, the rate of North American hosting may continue declining to only hosting one (6.7 percent) or two (13.3 percent) Games in future thirty-year periods.

Now much of this, like anything, has to do with the external environment. Consider the increasing competition to host the Games and the concept of locational obligation. Isn't it likely the Middle East and Africa will soon borrow Rio's successful game plan?

And what about the loyalty of frequent bidding to show the IOC that a country truly wants the Games? Beijing bid previously before emerging victorious in 2008. Toronto, which bid for the 1996 and 2008 Games, is 0-for-2 (as are Paris and Madrid).

If we suggest hosting the Games is clearly tied to funding, corporate or government interest and medals won, one could argue the

USOC has a big challenge to keep its Olympic performance record as one of the top two countries in overall medals at each and every Games and winning the most medals ever in a fully contested Games (110 in Beijing).

Is this the end of the American empire if the U.S. doesn't perform at its normal level in Vancouver and London? What if forecasts come true and Canada wins the most medals in Vancouver following a decade of strategic investment through an innovative "Own the Podium" program led by the COC, its partners and the Canadian government? Wouldn't it be interesting if Canada carries the new North American Olympic flag and hosts again in 2020 or 2022?

Arguably, one could say America must persevere by continuing to bid, specifically in 2020. But, if the corporate advantage of having multiple TOP sponsors and the biggest broadcaster is minimized, the U.S. might see a leveling of the playing field.

For now, there is no problem. But if America starts dropping in the medal count, it may be a function of many small forces at play. You remember the old nursery rhyme, don't you? For want of the nail and shoe, the horse and rider were lost.

27

Consider Intangibles When Weighing Olympic Host-City Benefits

Published September 7, 2009

WE NOTED WITH GREAT INTEREST the recent announcement from the Chinese government in Beijing that it made $146 million in operating profit from hosting the 2008 Summer Olympic Games. This proclamation was notable insomuch as the outcome didn't suggest any forensic accounting had been conducted by an impartial third party. But that's the norm. Each city hosting the Olympics wants to show its citizens (or government) the pomp and circumstance didn't cost anyone anything. As Shakespeare might have said, "All's well that ends well . . . if we're profitable."

But there is much more to hosting the Olympic Games than simple cost accounting. Although varied views exist, and there is undeniably significant impact on a city beyond ticket sales, researchers still need to explore a variety of investments, including economic development, branding, volunteer training, facility legacies, health care improvements and more.

In the case of Beijing's Games, did BOCOG's investment strategy go beyond net profitability? Was it more important for the Games to showcase China's growing economy and tourism/branding than to improve the quality of life for Beijing residents? What is it really like in Beijing and the outlying districts one year later?

For many, the Chinese government probably succeeded on numerous levels, but scholars and journalists should still ask if bidding cities and their governments are fully considering the investment "quantum" of winning the Games. Are legacy programs or volunteerism vehicles more developed because the International Olympic Committee demands as much in the bid or because the organizing committee truly wanted to change social conditions for their huddled masses?

We fully understand this is treacherous political ground, and it explains why press releases stick to reporting profitability or, when the result was unprofitable, promoting infrastructure "leave-behinds" for the next generation. This is logical but limiting. For the benefit of future bidders, shouldn't someone focus on and aggregate the other impacts of the Games? If the answer is yes, what should happen next?

First, we should ask how Vancouver 2010, London 2012, Sochi 2014, and the four 2016 bidding cities of Chicago, Madrid, Rio de Janeiro and Tokyo can optimize their respective up-front investments.

In Vancouver, where 64 percent of citizens voted in favor of hosting the Games in a 2003 plebiscite, the Games have come under scrutiny for budget shortfalls necessitating a bailout loan of approximately $87 million (U.S.) and a recent request for around $20 million (U.S.) related to the construction of the Olympic village. (In Vancouver's case, the IOC has already announced it will financially help with—but not completely cover—VANOC's debts if there is a deficit following February's Winter Olympics.)

In London, news is emerging that forensic accountants are suggesting a massive shortfall (roughly $160 million, U.S.) in the London Development Agency's 2012 Olympics account. If accurate, that is one deep hole.

Shouldn't someone probe the issue of host-city investment logic/strategy going in and the real results coming out? Is there an overfocusing on costs and a lack of emphasis on long-term direct, indirect and intangible outcomes? Granted, Olympic impact measurement has been around for years, and both of us have previously written on it.

Many others have also conducted considerable research, yet the nut that is a true holistic review is still not cracked.

The challenge of unexpected cost overruns during construction, massive operating budgets and increasing media scrutiny as the Games approach is common. But when the Games cost billions to stage and then show a relatively slight profit or healthy loss, then the citizens of hosting cities deserve some form of independent "here's how we really benefited" findings two to five years later.

This is where we can learn from economists who study economic impact. Generally speaking and widely agreed upon, the impact of an event is calculated under three distinct areas: (1) direct financial impacts (e.g., jobs created to build facilities, visitors related to the Games, etc.); (2) indirect financial impacts (e.g., tourism incremental gains due to Games, long-term job growth, etc.); and (3) intangibles (e.g., improved volunteer base, stronger city brand, healthier population, etc.).

Clearly, measuring direct impacts is easier; however, it is possible to measure or estimate the indirect and intangible impacts.

There is also the issue of "unit of analysis." Do we measure impact by the organizing committee, the city, the province/state or the country? Or all of them collectively? For example, in Barcelona (1992), the Spanish government was reportedly left a $6.1 billion (all figures U.S.) debt despite the organizing committee reporting a profit of $3 million.

Similarly, in Nagano (1998), reports suggested the Olympic committee showed a $28 million profit, but various government groups were left with $11 billion in debt. Some Games do not differentiate, such as Albertville (1992), which reportedly lost $57 million, and Atlanta (1996) and Sydney (2000), who both reported breaking even.

In consideration of intangible benefits, can we actually say Atlanta only broke even? Is Atlanta a bigger, better, more respected global city for having hosted the 1996 Games? Is it higher on people's to-visit list when they consider a holiday? Was the city's thrill at hosting Australians, Austrians and Argentineans ever measured? Is their population healthier? Did the city secure a better future?

A review of the published plans for Vancouver, London, Sochi, Chicago, Madrid, Rio de Janeiro and Tokyo portrays considerable attention to legacy aspects, ranging from facilities to volunteerism to health outcomes. However, these aspects and others of interest need to be enhanced and evaluated conservatively with appropriate metrics, clear benchmarks and long-term data collections. And done so independently well after the circus has rolled up its tent and left town.

Further, we think evaluations of the Olympic Games bidders and hosts should not be based solely on costs and cost overruns, but on the holistic outcomes generated. Evaluations must go beyond dollars and scratch at what hosting the Games really does to a city and then help bidding cities articulate what they want the Games to do for them.

PART THREE

Looking at How Things Are Done in Canada and around the Globe

28

How to Bridge the Sports Research–Practitioner Divide

Published January 21, 2013

AS A *SPORTSBUSINESS JOURNAL* READER, you're likely aware of the expanding number of university sport management programs, the rising flood water of graduates looking for jobs and the vague role of professors as teachers and researchers. Many of you could be unaware that for most tenured (or tenure-track) professors, research is their primary activity and not teaching.

Research, you may say, why would I care about that? We posed that very question.

In December, at the Sport Management Association of Australia and New Zealand's annual conference in Sydney, one of us was asked to give a three-minute speech on a topic of choice, knowing that one of Australia's top practitioners would respond to our critique. Since we both were there, we huddled and created a potentially provocative topic: Why isn't the academic sport management community (and its scholarly research output) more relevant to the sports industry?

To paraphrase a familiar movie line, we wanted to provoke discussion by essentially saying, "Research? We don't need no stinking research."

That's not to say there aren't exceptions. UEFA, Europe's most important soccer league, has a robust grant program (entering its fourth edition) that encourages scholars to generate new initiatives in European football research. And the NFL, America's largest sporting league, has enjoyed a long-standing relationship with Stanford University professor George Foster to facilitate its in-house executive education.

But unlike what we see with the medical profession or via business CEOs, where published research in publications like the *New England Journal of Medicine* or *Harvard Business Review* are snapped up by active practitioners, sports industry executives seem comfortable believing only active practitioners can articulate anything worth knowing about the sports business. This seems unfortunate, particularly since numerous university researchers are working on cutting-edge developments in sports, many tied to former professionals (who now happen to teach).

It's important recognizing this academic–practitioner divide in sports management is notable despite massive growth on both fronts over the past decade. This gap, probably driven by trust and performance, is real.

On the academic side, there are more than 1,000 sport management programs worldwide, each with its own set of courses and professors. As the field formalizes, the number of outlets for published research now includes 10 peer-reviewed journals specific to the field and hundreds of others in sports marketing, finance, psychology, economics, law and others that publish regularly. Similarly, the practitioner side has seen considerable growth in the number and complexity of jobs involved.

Sports organizations now seek out trained professionals—former athletes or not—who have specific and specialized skills in areas like sponsorship, finance, human resources, marketing and operations.

So, why the gap relative to research? There are clearly examples of strong interaction between research and practice. But the culture of sports and academics in North America is a long way from other disciplines and fields in terms of synergy or integrating with each other.

So, why aren't more practitioners reading *Sport Marketing Quarterly* or the *Journal of Sport Management*? Is it because the academics who write papers for these journals have made their work so hard to understand (or so nuanced in what was researched) that the average practitioner can't see any value? Is the writing so dense that the key points are obscured?

Or is the issue a communications one? Is it too expensive or time-consuming to find and read articles in journals like the *International Journal of Sport Finance* or the *European Sport Management Quarterly*? Are the articles too slow to hit print?

Or are we—the professors—actually the problem? Are we so focused on case studies, concepts and guest lecturers in our classes that we fail to properly convey the value that exists in our literature to our students in professional programs? In our experiences, we provide our thesis/honors students with a strong grounding and background in the literature, but students like that typically become professors. In our practitioner-focused classes, the peer-review stuff tends to take a back seat.

Perhaps a cultural shift in our field is needed if we're to narrow this gap and continue to achieve reliable credibility.

Here's an interesting case to illustrate: One of us is the former North American editor of a peer-reviewed journal designed specifically to link academics and industry around the topic of sponsorship. Then, despite four years of strong scholarship, good reviews, high levels of interest from submitting authors, a strong editorial board of global academics and practitioners, plus popular topics, the journal had to be partnered with another journal as readership and subscriptions were below sustainable levels.

So what to do? We suggested in Sydney that academic organizations look to create clearinghouses of academic experts or, at the very least, design a protocol whereby active research (or recently published work) can be placed in front of leading industry professionals. If the research is valid and shared in a nonthreatening way, we should see some traction.

But the alternative is what bothers us. What if we have an industry that doesn't care about the research emanating from thousands of academic professionals? What if we have an industry that is so certain about itself that it purposely ignores the research done on its behalf? It's a scary thought and one we hope to change.

29

Grey Cup's Centennial Should Have Marketers Taking Notice

Published November 12, 2012

THE SUPER BOWL is the undisputed single-day champion of annual sports television ratings in North America. With a worldwide TV audience of more than 150 million and network advertising revenue approaching $4 million per 30-second spot, it's an American event of unparalleled proportions.

But what if we asked you to name North America's top five? Would you guess the World Series? The NBA All-Star Game? The Indy 500? What about the NFL's conference championship games?

While it's not quite a clear-cut answer (based on teams involved, date or year), we're comfortable framing an argument that one of the right answers is an annual football game staged north of the U.S. border by the Canadian Football League. We know that because in 2011 the CFL's Grey Cup continued its decade-long rise as a Super Bowl-esque event that comes close to stopping a nation. To wit, this Cup (and not Lord Stanley's) is widely known for drawing avid fans from across an entire country to a weeklong, citywide celebration.

With the CFL's TV audience peaking, according to BBM Canada, at 14 million Canadians for the TSN (English) and RDS (French) broadcasts, and sponsorship support growing (reportedly up 16 per-cent for 2011), including investments from brands like Nissan, Molson Canada and Scotiabank, the Grey Cup's performance is quite compa-rable to the NFL's conference championship games. Even better, the Grey Cup's total reach via TV was about 42 percent of Canada's 34 million population, and penetration numbers like that suggest that the Cup in Canada is similar to the Super Bowl's relevance in the U.S.

"It's not a particularly favorable economy right now, but the Argo-nauts have done quite well with our partnership revenue numbers," said Dave Bedford, who is leading the sales and marketing for the Toronto Argonauts' management of the 2012 Grey Cup Festival, the historic 100th. "As of Oct. 10, we had 41 sponsors, a multistation television and radio partnership, and two major daily newspaper part-nerships. We're ahead of plan in terms of cash, budget-relieving VIK [value-in-kind or contra sponsorship] and non-budget-relieving tar-gets. We're also significantly ahead of any previous Grey Cup Festivals . . . which really isn't a surprise given the significance of the Grey Cup centennial and the fact it's taking place in Canada's biggest market."

Bedford went on to describe the vast cityscape of celebrations hap-pening around Toronto by noting, "What's really interesting about these Grey Cup activations is that we have four specific zones of activ-ity that are all demographically based or linked to specific target mar-kets such as family, teens, partiers, football fans and others."

Each zone carries the name of a sponsor—for example, Nissan, MBNA, Telus and Scotiabank—and is located in downtown Toronto at familiar locations such as Yonge-Dundas Square, Nathan Phillips Square/City Hall and the Metro Toronto Convention Centre. At the MBNA Adrenaline Zone for young adults, the *Toronto Sun* will even go so far as to present the world's longest urban zip line.

Strangely, though, most American sports marketers rarely know when or where the Grey Cup is held and may not know if their brand should start thinking about the value of this event in order to leverage Canadian activation opportunities. Perhaps the CFL needs to up its marketing efforts south of the border in places like Buffalo, Detroit,

Cleveland, Columbus, and Syracuse, where football fans are many and sport marketers are among the most sophisticated in the world.

For starters, the Grey Cup is thought to have created about $118 million of economic impact in Vancouver for 2011's three-day festival. That $100 million-plus would approach the NBA's All-Star Game this past February in Orlando, which reportedly brought in about 50,000 out-of-town visitors, booked more than 25,000 room nights and attracted more than 1,000 media members (many of them from foreign countries).

Further, the Grey Cup gives Canadians something the NHL can't: an eight-team league filled only with Canadian teams (not to mention a league that isn't locked out). Given that the NHL has canceled all November games, this 100th Cup should attract an even larger audience and raises the question of whether NHL sponsors were looking for the right contingency alternatives a year ago.

So, in case you're wondering: This year's Cup will take place at the Rogers Centre in Toronto on Nov. 25, but the festival itself will cover nine days (beginning Saturday and running through game day), and CFL Commissioner Mark Cohon thinks this year could be a breakthrough year. Given the tribal relationship between fans and football, it should be.

"Nothing brings Canadians together quite like the Grey Cup," Cohon said. "The festival revolves around the game, but the game has evolved into a celebration of our league, our country and the bond between them."

That sounds like an executive who knows his regional/national brand now acts very much like a global property. What a shame that some American sports marketers don't realize what's happening less than 100 miles from their border.

30

Reasons to Believe in India Football League

Published November 21, 2011

AS WRITERS AND RESEARCHERS, we spend an inordinate amount of time following information related to sports business. One item that got our attention in August was about football taking off in India. It's a story you might have even mentioned to your friends.

"The Elite Football League of India," you said with a hint of cynicism. "American investors trying to build an eight-team NFL-style football league in India starting in November 2012."

I'm sure that will happen.

But you didn't mean it. Even though former NFL stars Ron Jaworski and Michael Irvin and former Chicago Bears coach Mike Ditka were reportedly involved. That's because you conjured up some outdated image of India and couldn't see American football catching on over there. The Hyderabad Skykings and Goa Swarm? C'mon, get real.

And yet the eye-opener in that Indian football announcement was the broad suggestion the league would grow to 52 teams by 2022. Yes, 52 teams—20 more than the NFL.

It sounds crazy until you consider India is on pace to become the world's most populated country with more than triple the population of the U.S. and Canada combined. India is also developing an upper and middle class at a rapid clip, so the supply of potential owners and season-ticket buyers is considerable. You're still kidding, right?

Well, we wonder how you felt when you first heard about Brazil bidding to host the 2014 FIFA World Cup and 2016 Summer Olympic Games in a single two-year period. Or learned China was attempting to build a major pro basketball empire while pulling off the largest Olympic Games to date?

For many of us, our old-school parochial nature (maybe it's even a bit jingoistic) keeps us from accepting that China, Brazil and India feature booming economies and massive population segments looking for entertainment options. Think of North America in the 1950s: growing, changing, prospering and expanding.

Don't get caught up believing that another global superpower can't possibly take a good idea and build something new and improved. Countries like India, Korea and China have done it in other industries—technology, automotive, service—so why not sports? Plus, football provides a weekly special event for fans other sports can't match due to voluminous schedules and longer seasons.

It also provides a championship game unmatched in its singular ability to attract attention as a festival. These hospitality facts haven't gone unnoticed around the globe.

Perhaps you're recalling the NFL's experience in Europe and pondering whether investors so lustily eyeing India will end up wasting their money. After all, there are intelligent NFL owners still grumbling about how much they spent propping up teams like the Barcelona Dragons, Frankfurt Galaxy and Scottish Claymores.

But give us this: Times change, technology improves, and today's global sport managers are more sophisticated. The success of India's IPL (professional cricket), despite some challenges, is a multibillion-dollar league leveraging an international broadcast deal with YouTube.

Additionally, a market of ticket-paying, merchandise-buying sports fans exists and grows daily as India become more urban, more educated and more developed. And don't worry about whether India has enough stadiums for football. With the construction efforts that

supported the 2010 Commonwealth Games, India already has 13 stadiums of 50,000 seats or more in cities such as New Delhi, Kochi,
Kolkata, Mumbai, and Bangalore. In Kolkata alone, Salt Lake Stadium (120,000) and Ranji Stadium (90,000) would dwarf most NFL
stadiums in the U.S.

As we approach November 2012, we know your doubts about
India will remain. But you have to admit the potential is interesting,
and Americans have bet on crazier stock plays before. Hollywood and
our technology sector invest heavily in India daily. So, keep your skepticism but make sure you aren't too smug about NFL-style football
on the subcontinent.

31

Results of Canadian Sponsorship Study Relevant for Everyone

Published August 22, 2011

IN CONJUNCTION with the Formula One race in Montreal in early July, we were invited to speak at the seventh annual Canadian Sponsorship Forum. The forum is, by most accounts, Canada's top annual sponsorship conference, with three days of presentations, workshops, tremendous hospitality and a link to a spectacular major event. (In 2012, it will return to Montreal linked to the Just for Laughs comedy festival.)

An annual staple of the forum is the Canadian Sponsorship Landscape Study, which surveys sponsors; properties of all types (professional, amateur and grassroots sports, causes, events, festivals and entertainment); and agencies for their views, spending patterns and opinions on sponsorship trends over the past year and their forecasting of said trends for future years. Although the data is specific to the Canadian market and designed for Canadian marketers, there are some important findings that are relevant to readers in the U.S. and around the world. In some markets, there are comparable studies (e.g., *IEG Sponsorship Report* in the U.S.).

Indeed, with more than 400 companies responding on more than 50 variables in 2011, the data produced for the fifth annual version of the study provide an important and relevant perspective for Canadian Sponsorship Forum attendees. There are four specific points we believe are worth sharing with a broader North American audience.

First, in the last five years, the study has shown a 40 percent growth in sponsorship spending. Importantly, this includes the economic crisis of 2008 and 2009, when respondents of the third annual study (completed in early 2009) had expressed an expected 25 percent decline in spending. Although 2008 was a lower growth year than others (which have trended around 10 percent normally), sponsorship still grew modestly, despite marketing budgets overall decreasing. Said another way, the ability and effectiveness of sponsorship in cluttered environments was and continues to be clearly demonstrated in a period of constrained spending.

Second, although it is clear that sponsors and property organizations are more committed than ever when it comes to articulating evaluation and proof of sponsorship effectiveness, they are not putting their money where their mouth is. Less than 5 percent of sponsorships are evaluated, and only a fraction of those are structured evaluations with benchmarks for measurement set pre-sponsorship. The conundrum is that across all three stakeholder groups, sponsorship practitioners express an overwhelming desire for better evaluation, improved ROI assessments and proof. In the advertising world, that metric has always been as simple as stating CPM or a ratings guarantee. To wit, either an ad delivered against a targeted demographic, or the programming reached the minimum number of households set by the broadcaster. In sponsorship, the formula is more complex. In either case, there has rarely been a conclusive or open discussion on whether the creative worked or whether customers changed their buying habits. Sponsorship requires a more custom approach. According to respondents, we have that ability but now must follow through and allocate budget to implement.

Third, there continues to be a problem with many companies not providing enough activation to support their initial sponsorship investment. This was perhaps the most controversial point in the study results because the sponsorship-to-activation spending ratio of 1 to 1,

2 to 1 or, on the low side, 0.5 to 1 was brought up. It was suggested that Canadian sponsors activate less than their American, Australian or British counterparts, but this was debated in some corners on the accuracy of the numbers used in creating these ratios (i.e., what is included in a rights fee differs from study to study, from respondent to respondent). That said, across large samples of data, one can assume these errors all cancel out, so we're comfortable to say that Canadians are under-activating. Regardless and most important as a takeaway is the point that sponsors (and properties to some extent) need to activate more in Canada. As George Orwell might have suggested in his seminal work *Animal Farm*, it appears all sponsors are created equally, but some are more equal than others when it comes to activation.

Fourth, property servicing remains far below sponsor expectations on a variety of metrics. This is perhaps less surprising on second review but is clearly tied to the price-value challenge every sponsor faces. Also, putting data behind this point was very illustrative and had conference attendees' eyes popping. In reality, property organizations are facing increases across the board in costs and are asking for ever-increasing dollars. Sponsors are paying those dollars and extracting their ounce (or gallon/liter) of blood from the property but still protesting that they are not serviced the way they expect. To that end, property organizations are slowly learning to assign more account representatives at a time when boards and CEOs are calling for layoffs and using the always handy expression that "We'll just need to do more with less." The reality is that sponsors have the right to push properties to provide more for less. Sponsors have the money, and there are always other properties in which to invest.

"The issue of maximizing and measuring sponsorship ROI is often too narrowly considered," said Mark Harrison, president of sports marketing agency TrojanOne and founder of the Canadian Sponsorship Forum. "But it needs to be evaluated across all related marketing activities, including activation touch points pre-, during and post-event. The real issue, though, is not only having the data the study provides, but getting stakeholders to use it to their advantage to validate their proposals, servicing and/or activation plans. If they don't, they're going to fall behind the curve of an industry that's only getting smarter."

The final report of the Canadian Sponsorship Landscape Study was set to be released last Friday. It endeavors to dig deeper and provide guidelines for sponsors, properties and agencies per Harrison's important recommendation.

32

Resurgence Changing How Sports World Views Canadian Market

Published February 28, 2011

OFTEN OVER THE PAST 20 YEARS, many of us would have argued professional sport in Canada was in crisis. Only Toronto seemed immune. For those who tend not to look northward, here are a few memory joggers:

• The NBA's Grizzlies left Vancouver for Memphis.

• The MLB's Expos bounced from Montreal to Washington, D.C.

• The NHL's Nordiques and Jets took off from Quebec City and Winnipeg for Colorado and Phoenix, respectively. Three other Canadian NHL teams—the Calgary Flames, Edmonton Oilers and Ottawa Senators—each came close to financial failure and teetered on the edge of extinction. At one point, even the storied Montreal Canadiens were reportedly under water, 26 Stanley Cups notwithstanding!

• MLB's Toronto Blue Jays were usually no better than mediocre. In fact, the Jays haven't won their division since 1993 and finished fourth in their five-team American League division the last three consecutive years.

• The CFL launched an ambitious expansion into the United States only to retract two years later.

• The CFL's Ottawa franchise folded twice, and Montreal went under once. These are cities of 1 million and 3.5 million people, respectively.

• The Formula One race in Montreal, North America's only F1 event and reportedly the third-most-watched television event in the world in 2005, was shut down following the 2008 race and thought unlikely to return.

Looking back, it seemed like Canada, one-tenth the size, in population and market, of its big brother to the south, could not house pro franchises and non-Olympic mega-events at the highest level. Confidence was down, sport fans looked depressed, and Canadian owners were licking their fiscal wounds. Thoughts of an NHL with only two or three Canadian teams (plus the demise of the CFL) were not uncommon or unfounded.

Fast-forward to 2011, and the professional Canadian sports landscape is suddenly sparkling. A 180-degree turn, some might say. To illustrate, we present a few facts worth noting:

• After placing an MLS team in Toronto in 2007, a team standing out as one of the league's brightest lights off the field, Don Garber's expansion crew recently added teams in Vancouver (starting this year) and Montreal (2012).

• The CFL is doing well, heading back to Ottawa and making serious inquiries about expanding into eastern Canada. In fact, with the exception of Toronto, the CFL is experiencing some of its most notable success ever. The last two Grey Cups—Canada's Super Bowl—have drawn TV audiences in excess of 6 million viewers, record highs for the event.

• The Blue Jays hired general manager Alex Anthopoulos, a Greek Canadian, after the 2009 season. Anthopoulos is thought by many to be one of the sharpest young general managers in the game, and, perhaps not surprisingly, the Jays finished 2010 eight games over .500 and produced a dynamic off-season in preparation for 2011.

• While the NHL is now struggling in the southern U.S., there is much attention and interest focused on the league possibly returning to Winnipeg, Quebec City or both. In fact, Canada's leading sport network, TSN, and its sport business correspondent, David Naylor, presented a six-part series last June outlining the business case for the return of the NHL to Manitoba and Quebec and a second team for the Toronto area. *Hockey Night in Canada*, the country's most-watched regular sports program, presented a similar piece last December.

• The F1 race is back in Montreal (the Ferraris and McLarens hit the Gilles Villeneuve Circuit in early June), and the Canadian Sponsorship Forum will run at the same time as the F1 race.

• Ongoing rumors, innuendo and hints of truth continue to suggest that two and possibly four NFL teams might be considering moving into Toronto, North America's fourth-largest market and a city with a growing regional population racing toward 9 million. The Buffalo Bills have signed a multiyear deal to play a total of eight preseason and regular-season games in the Rogers Centre over a five-year span.

Wonder why the Canadian turnaround is so pronounced?

We can give some credit to a strong Canadian dollar (the loonie is now on par with the U.S. greenback) and a strong Canadian economy that felt the U.S. financial sector implosion much less severely. Also, a growing number of Canadian billionaires place Canadian professional sports in perhaps its strongest position ever.

If we mix in a successful Vancouver 2010 Winter Olympics and ongoing discussions of Toronto bidding for the 2020 Summer Olympics, we might find Canada is emerging as an attractive place for sport industrialists to ply their trade and generate acceptable margins.

But what does that mean to American sponsors and league administrators? Should they approach Canada as just a flavor of the month? Or should they think about buying into a country that has performed admirably when it comes to integrating sponsor support and growing passionate fan bases?

In an era of globalization, we all may need to view the sports market as North America rather than just the U.S.

33

What Americans Can Learn from Sports Day in Canada

Published December 20, 2010

ONE OF THE MOST SPECTACULAR and inspiring sports moments of 2010 was Sidney Crosby sliding the puck past American goalie Ryan Miller to win the Vancouver Winter Olympics ice hockey gold medal for the Canadians. That moment was every holiday wish come early for Canadians young and old.

But what if "les Canadians" wanted to give another gift to the United States that didn't involve heartache and dejection? What if for Christmas, Hanukkah, and Kwanzaa, Canada gave the U.S. a humble Boxing Day present that could truly benefit Americans and American sport industrialists?

The gift, presented here as just a simple idea, is Sports Day in Canada, and it's not a difficult concept to grasp. In fact, it demonstrates that effective nationalistic sport projects can be nationwide but still grassroots in their orientation.

Concepts like this are commonly built in other countries around mega-events like the Olympic Games and the FIFA World Cup. But grassroots activations using a country theme can be as simple as Soccer Day or Basketball Day. They don't need a mega-event, just a commitment from a group like the U.S. Olympic Committee or even the White House. They just need vision.

In the case of Sports Day in Canada, that passion came from ParticipACTION, a well-known nonprofit advocate for physical activity and sport participation in Canada supported by the Canadian government and corporate partners.

Building on the concept of previous Canadian TV–driven events like Hockey Day and Soccer Day, Sports Day in Canada was held for the first time in September, with Canadian organizations and citizens from coast to coast encouraged to host or join in sports and physical-activity events. Events took place between Sept. 11 and 18, culminating with six hours of national television coverage. The CBC (and its French sister station, Radio-Canada) partnered on the program with a full day of coverage including programming on triathlon, swimming, rugby, para sport, gymnastics, basketball, and swimming, as well as one-hour shows specific to Sports Day called *What Moves Canada* and *What Moves Canada's Kids*.

"The first Sports Day in Canada built off the magic of the 2010 Olympics and Paralympics to galvanize the sport sector around a common purpose," said Kelly Murumets, president and CEO of ParticipACTION. "Not only did we register over 1,000 local celebration events in communities across the country, we saw over 1.25 million Canadians join us as spectators or participants. We mobilized national, regional, local, broadcast, sport, media, sponsor, and government partners who wore their hearts on their sleeves—in a way that benefited each individual organization as well as the sector as a whole."

So how did it work?

It had a champion with a great brand and credibility.

ParticipACTION, thanks to a memorable campaign in the 1980s, was reborn in 2007, six years after it ceased operating when its government funding was cut.

Since its rebirth, ParticipACTION had adopted and developed a diverse and successful funding model that included government funding, partnerships and fund-raising. In addition to CBC and Radio-Canada, partners involved in Sports Day in Canada included True Sport,

Canadian Soccer Association, Canadian Olympic Committee, IMI International Research, Canadian Paralympic Committee, Canadian Centre for Ethics in Sport and the Coaching Association of Canada.

"Partnerships for Sports Day in Canada were more than just components of an inaugural funding model. Securing strategic partnerships with national voices like CBC, True Sport, the COC and CPC were vital platforms to effectively promote community engagement at a grassroots level," said Mark Harrison, president of TrojanOne, the agency engaged in the development of Sports Day in Canada. "The equity Sports Day in Canada gained through partnerships allowed the movement to steep its roots deep into communities across Canada and deliver inspirational stories that got Canadians moving."

A long-term integrated promotion perspective was taken.

The 2011 version is already in the works, and concepts like Jersey Day increased attention. Held Sept. 17, Canadians were asked to show support for sport by wearing a jersey, team or club uniform to school, work or play.

"Jersey Day is a very important element of the entire Sports Day in Canada campaign," Harrison said. "It's a simple premise, but it forges a highly visible collective action, anticipation, and ultimately awareness. Whether it drives a themed civvies day at your local school or turns your office into a sea of throwback jerseys, it generates a good PR story and allows Canadians to make the day theirs, whether at work or play."

Timing and activation are critical.

Sports Day in Canada followed just months after the very successful Vancouver Olympics, and that timing found Canadians still basking in a sense of pride for their country. For Americans, pride in sports events, teams and athletes is entrenched, and top sporting performances common. It is a matter of leveraging this pride through well-timed and supported grassroots activations.

So there you have it. A holiday gift sent south by the folks who are quietly taking a proactive stance on countrywide sport participation. Wonder if the Americans will want to play with this gift when they get their hands around it?

34

Assessing Vancouver after Facts, Accusations, Shades of Truth

Published August 30, 2010

YOU MAY RECALL almost a year ago when we chided Beijing bureaucrats for glibly announcing the 2008 Olympic Games reportedly made a tidy operating profit of $146 million. We were concerned then about the challenges of assessing true economic impact for a mega-event, the traditional underestimation of "legacy" intangibles and the "circus politics" of these reports.

Well, Vancouver 2010's turn to pontificate is imminent, and, although you'll likely hear different, we're confident VANOC and the city of Vancouver lost money but gained equity. In fact, we think, based on information trickling out of Lausanne, Switzerland, that the International Olympic Committee is sufficiently prepared to help compensate VANOC for revenue losses tied to the shattered global economy (2008–10) and pre-Games weather.

Driving this issue is a little-read report given to the Vancouver City Council (heard in late April and based on preliminary data) suggesting that after the Canadian and British Columbia governments picked up a tab of about $175 million (all figures Canadian), the estimated bill for Vancouver would approach, if not exceed, $600 million.

In simple terms, the morning-after economic indicators are clearly pointing south.

But what if various Vancouver parties did lose money? Is that all bad? Our assessment: It isn't. That's because the cost of building things or growing city reputations can't always be booked as losses. As we noted previously, never underestimate the future economic value of intangibles like city pride and volunteerism or the indirect benefits like tourism and brand enhancement. But start with this: If economists were given full access to all Vancouver data, they would likely suggest Vancouver did well from a capital perspective although the city's cash-flow analysis and projections were ugly.

Additionally, the fact that none of Vancouver's capital benefits (highways, athletic facilities, social housing, etc.) and intangible gains would have happened when they did without the procurement of the Games is important here. How we determine the value of these benefits drives how independent parties view Vancouver's economic success or failure.

Third, relatively speaking, debt of $600 million, amortized over the long term, is not horrific. Although the city had to take over the athletes village project when its original financier pulled out (thought to be about $1 billion), you must remember Vancouver was Canada's third Olympic Games in 34 years. That gives us two extreme precedents:

• Conservative Calgary, at one end of the spectrum, enjoyed estimated profits in the neighborhood of $100 million, not including government-funded infrastructure projects, which funded many initiatives and grew as an endowment under the Calgary Olympic Development Association.

• Manic Montreal sits at the other end with an estimated debt of $1 billion. Its legacy includes numerous facilities that hung like albatrosses around the city's sagging neck.

But if we benchmark versus other Olympic cities, there are marketing positives to infer. Think of the benefits of putting a city on the map for tourism and economic development (e.g., Sydney, Atlanta) or building unprecedented awareness for a ski resort region (e.g., Lake Placid, Albertville).

City branding as a concept is now well-established and holds the potential to offer long-term benefits for many municipalities, although quantifying is difficult and expensive. Contemporary scholars know this and are working on research showing how sponsors can indirectly benefit from strong city branding via mega-event management.

Finally, as hinted above, keep in mind Vancouver's budget assessment is only one piece of the budget equation. Three other organizations pitched in considerably. The final numbers of VANOC, the province and the federal government are not yet out. Their budgets were $1.75 billion, $763 million and $898 million, respectively. Combined, that's $3.41 billion invested in a region that features a great ski destination, one NHL team and one MLS expansion unit (the Whitecaps start play in 2011).

"It's all fabulous but it was very, very expensive," said Vancouver City Councilor Geoff Meggs in comments published in April by the (Toronto) *Globe and Mail*. "The largest part is in the capital costs, and it cost more than it should have. There was no budget control under the [previous] administration."

Vancouver City Councilor Suzanne Anton suggested Meggs was missing the point. She told the *Globe and Mail*, "The report makes the expenses look exceptionally high because the city's budget office included every project completed in advance of the Olympics, even if it was already on the books to be done."

Wars with words are born in the reality of casual economics. As soon as a city wins a major event bid that requires construction (i.e., the Olympics), the cost of concrete, cranes and crowbars doubles and triples. Why? The simple answer is massive locked-in demand, specialized suppliers and limited supply. Add to that an immovable deadline and global scrutiny, and it's a foreman's dream.

To that end, we looked to the cities of Calgary (1988), Albertville (1992), Nagano (1998), and Salt Lake City (2002)—all in comparable locations to Vancouver. In each case, the local organizing committee broke even or reported a modest profit. However, in all but Salt Lake City, government bodies kicked in substantially for infrastructure.

Despite numerous challenges, we've mixed art with forecasting science to suggest VANOC will ultimately announce a profit of $29 million, not including the capital investments in roads, stadiums, etc. (which we are assuming as a break-even for the city).

So there you have it . . . we sat on the fence. We've reported the city of Vancouver "lost" money but believe VANOC will announce a "profit" just to make sure the politics of the circus remain friendly.

Call it modern sports economics at work.

35

NHL Must Be Strong on Power Plays of Innovation, Globalization

Published February 22, 2010

WHEN THE NHL HIT BOTTOM a few years back with a painful lockout that cost the league its 2004–5 season, many thought the sport was doomed or, at the very least, in for some very tough times. What followed were NHL attendance levels that not only bounced back (for the second time after a lockout) but surpassed pre-lockout levels (see chart below).

The league also has two young, electrifying superstars in Washington's Alexander Ovechkin and Pittsburgh's Sidney Crosby, a unique midseason event in the outdoor Winter Classic (most recently held at Fenway Park) and the powerful knowledge that the majority of its elite players are participating in the most anticipated ice hockey tournament in history.

So, let's cut to the chase: Do you know where you'll be on Sunday? We do.

Watching the men's Olympic gold-medal hockey game in Vancouver.

We also think it will be Canada vs. the United States, and the game will represent a sports watershed moment that rivals in importance the

6. Crowd at the 2014 Molson Canadian National Hockey League Face-Off. *Courtesy of Dave Sandford/NHLI via Getty Images.*

U.S.–Soviet Union "Miracle on Ice" of 1980 and the epic Canada–Soviet Union battles of the 1970s.

But whether we're right about the teams or the magnitude of the game, the reality is that hockey, particularly the NHL's brand of hockey, is taking center stage at these Vancouver Games. And it's taking that stage as a game once again on the move for two key reasons.

First, Commissioner Gary Bettman, now in his 17th year at the helm of the NHL, has been willing to shut down his league in midseason no less than four times to ensure the Olympics and its many TV networks see hockey at its finest.

Second, and one could insist that this point is a result, in part, of the first, is the rise of the game globally, particularly with the growth of professional hockey leagues in Europe. The Kontinental Hockey League, with 24 teams in Russia, Belarus, Latvia and Kazakhstan, continues to make noise. Teams there now average between 4,000 and 8,000 fans a game, and the KHL has attracted a number of top players, including former NHL MVP Jaromir Jagr.

Table 3. NHL Attendance (Includes Playoffs)

Season	Games	Attendance
1993–94	1,182	17,545,699
1994–95*	705	10,563,014
1995–96	1,152	18,581,754
1996–97	1,148	19,135,407
1997–98	1,148	18,722,094
1998–99	1,193	19,511,152
1999–2000	1,231	20,324,768
2000–2001	1,316	21,957,390
2001–02	1,320	22,305,787
2002–03	1,319	22,044,824
2003–04	1,319	22,064,890
2004–05**	0	0
2005–06	1,313	22,384,574
2006–07	1,311	22,358,288
2007–08	1,315	22,823,309
2008–09	1,317	23,114,825

* Lockout resulted in the loss of 468 regular-season games.
** Lockout resulted in cancellation of season.
Source: *NHL Official Guide & Record Book* (Chicago: Triumph Books, 2009).

The NHL, for its part, has seen its total attendance jump, based on data gleaned from the annual *NHL Official Guide & Records Book*, from an average of 16,616 in the four-year period before the lockout (2000–4) to an average of 17,158 for the four-year period of 2005–9. This represents about a 3 percent increase. And, to boot, 2008–9 was the highest total attendance (nearly 21.5 million) for the league and was the fifth straight year of an increase.

So what does the NHL do from here, you ask? In our view, we would recommend four power plays to the commissioner:

1. Stay the course on the Olympic Games and go to Russia in 2014. We know there is more than meets the eye on this discussion and the coming collective-bargaining agreement discussions with the players association will need to address this matter. We also understand the absolute disruption the Olympics create for a daily business like the NHL.

2. Keep building on innovative and brand-building properties like the Winter Classic. Your staff is undoubtedly creative, and we think there are more new events to build that combine sponsor hospitality/ benefits and a "made-you-look" nature to the NHL's 82-game grind.

3. Keep close tabs on the KHL and keep globalization at the top of your 10-year forecast. We know distance and risk are there, but soccer players travel the world, and no reward comes without risk taken. Granted, the European stadiums make this economically difficult, but our point is driven by the projected visibility the Olympics will continue to provide the NHL.

4. Leverage all of this wonderful hockey attention to increased viewership and a bigger TV deal. We continue to believe digital TV and other digital media platforms (so critical to the communications dialogue with people younger than 30) will continue to give the fastest game the fastest chance to break back into a larger mainstream.

Are we hockey fans? Yes. With our respective Canadian heritages, it is in our DNA. But as observers of the sports business, we also have to holler when we see something notable.

36

Why Canada's Paint the Town Red Program Looks Like a Winner

Published January 18, 2010

WITH THE VANCOUVER WINTER OLYMPIC GAMES now less than a month away and the Canadian team poised to possibly lead the world in total medals, we thought it worthwhile to investigate the Canadian Olympic Committee's distinctive activation program, Paint the Town Red. It is a unifying marketing and operations concept that has already generated more than 32 million impressions and is actively benefiting Canadian athletes and sponsors alike.

But what, you ask, does an effective Olympic activation really involve?

1. There must be something of value to activate upon.

As hinted above, Canadian winter sport athletes, thanks in part to Canada's Own the Podium performance program, are placing at or near the top in recent winter World Cups or World Championships. That's significant because Canada is the only country ever to host the Olympic Games (Montreal 1976 and Calgary 1988) and not win a gold medal.

2. Strong activation also calls for an integrated (i.e., multi-platform) approach.

In the case of Paint the Town Red, this includes a national public relations campaign, newsletters (online and print), videos at professional sport venues (and all 2010 Olympic Torch Relay celebrations), co-promotions with sponsors, television advertising, out-of-home advertising (including 10 tractor trailers crisscrossing the country decorated in Paint the Town Red graphics), interactive activities, experiential marketing (street teams at Games time, partnering with CTV for celebrations), social media, an attractive website and creative signs.

3. Grassroots efforts are essential.

Here, the Canadian Olympic Committee has included its Canadian Olympic School Program that will deliver a Web-based Paint the Town Red activity guide for teachers and students (www.olympic school.ca) that will enable classrooms to follow and track the success of Canada's athletes in a values-based educational format. Also, the committee has engaged its partners in targeting grassroots efforts nationwide, not just in Vancouver.

"We have communities across Canada getting their citizens involved in Paint the Town Red," said David Bedford, the Canadian Olympic Committee's executive director of marketing and communications. "For instance, the Olympic host communities of Vancouver, Whistler and Richmond all have major community activations ongoing now, with more planned until the end of the Games. It is not just the Games cities, however, that are participating. Communities from all Canadian provinces are taking part—from big cities like Edmonton, Alberta, to smaller towns like Tweed, Ontario."

4. There must be infrastructure in place that allows the program to go viral.

This means an interactive microsite, Facebook and Twitter sites as well as content from the Canadian Olympic Committee corporate website. This has been exceptionally effective to date, as witnessed by the fully engaged Canadian Facebook community, which has quadrupled in size in the past month and was growing at a rate of 2.6 percent a day as of early January.

5. Getting numerous agencies involved helps maximize creativity and innovation.

For Paint the Town, the Canadian Olympic Committee used three agencies, for PR (Hill & Knowlton), creative (Hyphen Communications) and experiential (Inventa). The creativity of these groups has been notable, and an example is the Podium Pals program (www.podiumpals.olympic.ca), otherwise known as *chums de podium* in French. Podium Pals is an online tool that allows you to create a caricature of yourself (using an uploaded photo or photo from Facebook) doing your favorite winter Olympic sport.

Said Olympic freestyle skier Steve Omischl, "My strength has always been on skis, but Podium Pals allows me to take my Olympic aspirations to new heights—curling. Podium Pals is another way for Canadians to Paint the Town Red and support the Canadian Olympic Team. One thing that keeps me going on the road to 2010 is the knowledge that all of Canada is right behind me."

6. Perhaps most important is the need for both sponsor and property to activate their relationship and use customer thematics (see table).

As Bedford concedes, this is the first time they have launched efforts and invested in programs to build marketing equity for their sponsors (as opposed to spending money mostly on brand protection and leaving sponsors to create their own activation platforms).

"Paint the Town Red is a great platform from which to enhance our Olympic association," said Dave Struthers, director of promotion marketing and marketing communications at General Mills Canada. "With a giveaway like a T-shirt, Paint the Town Red provided the perfect thematic, and really cemented this program for us. Paint the Town Red took the T-shirt idea and made it real for consumers. This program was a huge success for us, from both a customer and consumer perspective."

In summary, it looks like the Canadian Olympic Committee has a hit on its hands with Paint the Town Red. Even better, the committee will be able to measure its effectiveness through the following vehicles:

• Number of impressions (paid media/advertising; earned media such as print coverage, online, sponsor reach, experiential reach, school program registration, social networks, etc.)

Table 4. Paint the Town Red Sponsor Activations

Sponsor	Activation Strategy
General Electric	Hold themed events at Robson Square skating rink, one for public prior to Games and one for family and friends during
McDonald's	Outfit restaurant staff in red uniforms, working to tie program into Paint the Town Red
Air Canada	In-flight entertainment to show Paint the Town Red video
Rona	Distributing 140,000 "Paintbook" tool kit booklets
Molson	Include Paint the Town Red logo/theme on key account programming during Games
General Motors	Sending Paint the Town Red tool kits to all dealers to promote theme
Acklands-Grainger	Paint the Town Red in customer catalogs
Workopolis	Include Paint the Town Red ad in newsletter to database of job searchers in November and February, reaching one million people
Insurance Corp. BC	Distribution of 100,000 "Paintbook" tool kits to customers in British Columbia
3M	Organized 10 tractor trailers crisscrossing Canada
Purolator	Distribution of 250,000 "Paintbook" tool kits to business customers
Sun Microsystems	Annual golf tournament themed as Paint the Town Red
VINCOR	Include theme in creative promotions to key accounts

Source: Canadian Olympic Committee.

• Research. Quantifiable measurements that reflect appropriate or planned improvements such as awareness or commitment to action. (It's worth noting that after the first eight weeks of the campaign, and without any paid media or experiential marketing, the program had reached 12 percent national awareness.)

• Legitimate testimonials from communities, individuals, teachers, coaches, athletic clubs, sponsors, etc.

The results to date suggest that Paint the Town (not to mention the country) Red is on the verge of becoming a nationwide social movement to inspire Canada to support its athletes as one country when it hosts the Vancouver Games in a few short weeks.

PART FOUR

Making the Sports World a Better Place

37

Rollerball Flashback: How Virtual Reality Replaces Violence

Published August 17, 2015

MANY PROFESSORS use films to illustrate key points in class or to support class materials. One of us annually shows YouTube clips from the 1975 movie classic *Rollerball,* and we wince every time we're obligated to watch director Norman Jewison imagining a more violent future for global sports. He didn't do it with human hunting (à la Richard Connell's "The Most Dangerous Game") but rather chose to place actor James Caan and others in football helmets and then made them chase each other around a banked oval on roller skates (or via motorcycles with grab rails).

At the end of the movie (spoiler alert here), the Rollerball world championship is conducted with no rules and no time limit. Essentially everyone but Caan dies. It wasn't the best screenplay ever, but the point behind violence in sports was clearly made: Win at all costs.

In thinking about this issue, we looked back and acknowledged the violence component was easy for the executive producers to pitch in Hollywood 40 years ago. It was the year of shock value, and hits like *Jaws, Death Race 2000, Dog Day Afternoon, The Ultimate Warrior,* and *Texas Chainsaw Massacre* (released in October 1974) populated the cinematic landscape. So, yes, there was a time when our culture thought violence (just like sex) sold. Many would suggest it still does.

But roller skates? Seriously?

Still, we were forced to salute Jewison's projection of a global sports league in 2018 (the suggested date of the movie), where Houston might play Madrid or Tokyo. And while it might have been nothing more than a one-off movie about the future, it reflected feelings some futurists held for sports as the 1970s hit their midpoint.

So flash-forward to the final exam for this particular class. Undergraduate college students are asked to extrapolate from course materials (including Nicholas Negroponte's brilliant book *Being Digital*) and predict the future triangulation of sports, media and society. Having spent a semester debating concepts and realities such as Oculus Rift, DraftKings, *Madden NFL 2015* (or *NBA 2K '15*), Spike Jonze's movie *Her*, the UFC, and CBS's *Survivor* (or Discovery Channel's *Naked and Afraid*), they are asked: "Forty years from now, what does sport in 2055 look like?"

Not an easy question for any of us.

Not surprisingly, many student answers projected significant growth in virtual and augmented reality. They could easily forecast the linkage between video games, fantasy sports, you-are-there graphics and player immersion (via teleportation). One young man wrote that sports in the middle of the 21st century "may include competition between teams that compete in virtual reality settings where pro clubs violently battle in a world that isn't actually real. The virtual reality piece allows for different locations, teams and many other variables that we [the viewer] can control."

The students already knew the new release of a video game can dwarf the revenue generated from a mainstream movie. *Grand Theft Auto V* reportedly reached $1 billion in sales in three days and *Call of Duty: Black Ops III* (set in 2065 and scheduled to be released Nov. 6) more than likely will surpass $2 billion this coming holiday season.

We understand that many in the sports industry don't think video games actually constitute "real" sports. And they shake their heads when they hear about professional gamers leveraging the digital universe and securing lucrative contracts from South Korean companies like LG and Samsung. We understand that DraftKings' market value a few months ago was roughly $900 million and that fantasy leagues will soon generate more than $5 billion annually in a spider web of reported and unreported cash flows.

Interestingly, in June, we started to get a glimpse of the future when leading sport management agency IMG announced its movement into eSports to focus on digital marketing and endorsement opportunities. Such a move by IMG signals a change in the sports industry, and while parent WME is not likely to abandon its bread and butter in talent representation, the old Boston Consulting Group marketing matrix for portfolio management (often called a "consultant's best friend") would suggest the "cash cows" of today are headed to "dogtown" and the "question marks" of yesterday will become the "stars" of tomorrow.

Frankly, we're not surprised. We hear this question about portfolio (or segment) growth on a weekly basis. Things are changing. Fast and furiously. The growing players now share content. They don't own it (think Google and Airbnb). And they cross-promote, cross-collaborate and cross-pollinate.

We've put forth answers to the media about fans wanting to experience sports from the comfort of their homes but expecting to be teleported into the middle of the offensive line in a football game, the scrum of a rugby contest or Centre Court at Wimbledon. They want to get down into the blocks just before the start of the Olympic final for the 100-meter dash.

James Caan might have been wearing a football helmet for a movie made in 1975 about 2018. The NFL was ascendant at that time, and Hollywood had already produced *The Longest Yard* (1974) and soon would offer up *Black Sunday* (1977) and *North Dallas Forty* (1979). Football was a safe bet, and America's disposable income would pour into NFL coffers for the next 40 years.

Today, though, we think you might want to quiz the young men and women entering your company at the lowest level. They might not have your Rolodex (or BlackBerry, iPad or Galaxy), but they might hold insight on questions you should start asking.

38

Top 10 List of Reasons Why the NCAA Still Matters

Published June 15, 2015

AS PROFESSORS, we're paid to read the tea leaves, and few days go by when the NCAA isn't the topic of discussion (usually critical), along with cynical blogs, click-bait blasts and stinging lawsuits. For lack of a better phrase, this association of nearly 1,300 colleges and universities is equal parts enigma and polarizing lightning rod.

But while we've seen a lot of negative flak fired at the 109-year-old NCAA about financial windfalls, educational purview and debates on athlete compensation, there's been little written about the coin's other side.

So we wanted to ask, Has the objectivity pendulum swung too far? Is it possible to turn the blowtorch down for one day and emphasize the NCAA's attributes? Can we write about holistic good (namely, that the organization helps more than 450,000 student athletes receive some form of financial assistance to attend institutions of higher learning) without appearing soft? Maybe.

So, in honor of David Letterman's retirement, we decided to present a top 10 list that shades the NCAA in a slightly different light:

10. The NCAA is the envy of the rest of the sporting world. While many of us critique and overanalyze the NCAA, the rest of the world

7. Ohio University student Brianna Reid poses at the Convocation Center. Students like Reid are essential to the future of the sports industry. *Courtesy of Ohio University.*

wants to emulate the American model of elite athletic development. Why? Because the NCAA is an unmatched sport development engine for elite athletes. Just ask anyone who works with young athletes from Australia, China or Canada. The U.S. Olympic Committee doesn't win anywhere near the 100 total medals it probably will score at the Brazil 2016 Summer Games without the NCAA.

9. The NCAA is the choice of many of America's largest sponsors. One of us was just part of a research team (led by Ron Seaver of the National Sports Forum and Jim Kahler of Ohio University) that presented findings from a study that interviewed 50 sponsors. More than a third (34 percent) said collegiate sports give them the biggest bang for their buck in sponsorship. That was the No. 1 result in the findings.

8. The NCAA is one of the top television properties in the United States. It is ESPN's No. 1 programming focus, with significant annual

dayparts allocated to football, basketball (both genders), lacrosse, baseball, hockey, and softball.

7. The football playoffs, held for the first time in 2015, were an unequivocal success: big ratings, big visibility and big payouts for numerous schools that offer hundreds of scholarships. We understand the conferences and College Football Playoff run the proceedings, not the NCAA, but those are NCAA athletes scoring those touchdowns, so we'll give the NCAA partial credit on this one.

6. The NFL, NBA, and WNBA all appreciate the NCAA's pre-developing of major brands like Marcus Mariota, Jahlil Okafor and Breanna Stewart. They also appreciate it was the NCAA who took on Indiana's Religious Freedom Restoration Act.

5. If the NCAA were broken up (or didn't exist), the economic laws of capitalism would reshape American sports in ways most practitioners can't imagine, and, we'd argue, that would mean fewer resources, less structure, less control and less success for many. In short, sports would become much more privatized and access to sports more costly.

4. There is no reason for the month of March without March Madness. Seriously. There is no NFL; the NBA and NHL are winding through their seasons still, not yet to the playoffs; MLB is in spring training; and MLS is just at the early part of its season. Heck, even NASCAR has already run its biggest race of the year and is left pointing toward its late-season elimination series.

3. There are now less than three months remaining until college football returns to various stadiums (large and small). You (as an individual) may not like football, but mainstream Americans really like college football. If you doubt us, check the numbers.

2. Few places in America are better than Baton Rouge on a Saturday night. Or Collegeville (Minn.) on a Saturday afternoon. Or Grand Forks (N.D.) when the Fighting North Dakotans are playing ice hockey. Or anywhere in Iowa during a collegiate wrestling dual. Or Indiana, Kentucky, North Carolina or Storrs (Conn.) when a basketball rivalry is heated. Or Utah when gymnastics is on.

1a. If it weren't for the NCAA, how often would Title IX have been discussed in the last 40 years? We dare say, a lot less.

8. Peden Stadium, home of the Ohio University football team, during a night game. *Courtesy of Ohio University.*

1. Did we say that the NCAA was the envy of the world? Yes, we want to emphasize this and give it the No. 1 spot. Every day in meeting rooms of the 200-plus other jurisdictions of the world where a national Olympic committee functions, we hypothesize the NCAA is mentioned with a jealous tone, such as "All our top athletes go there," or "If only our post-secondary system were like that."

We know it is fashionable to bash the NCAA. It is big, slow-moving and bureaucratic at times, even overly ambitious. But at the coalface, we continually see excitement created with each 10-0 Harvard football team and with each upset by a Wisconsin of an undefeated No. 1–ranked Kentucky. And we see the joy on the face of every collegian who was told in high school he or she wasn't good enough to play in college.

On the business side, we acknowledge there are issues with the operations and funding of college athletics, but we also ponder the alternatives. Would nearly half a million student athletes get to play high-level sports while being given the opportunity for a free (or reduced-cost) education without the NCAA? Would the high standing of colleges and universities in North American society drop by a noticeable amount if the NCAA didn't exist? (We think it would.)

So we'll end our rant here by asking a simple question for others to debate: Is it not better for fans to support universities (and show interest in higher education) than for them to shower approximately 140 professional team owners with more cash?

Discuss, and have your papers typed up by Thursday.

39

Are We Serious Enough about Diversity to Welcome All?

Published May 11, 2015

ONE OF US was recently invited to attend a scholarly conference in Hamburg, Germany, and what made this event particularly interesting was that the presentations from various academicians and practitioners took place outside along the concrete concourse of Millerntor-Stadion, the FC St. Pauli football complex.

But even more interesting than discussing marketing concepts with international guests was hearing that FC St. Pauli, housed in the shadows of former Nazi command bunkers and the famed Reeperbahn (where the Beatles first played), was using diversity—actually, was leveraging diversity—as a means to sell more tickets and team merchandise.

Make no mistake about the quality of FC St. Pauli. It is a team in the second division of German football/soccer and rarely moves up to the elite Bundesliga, which has the highest average per game attendance of any global league after the NFL.

Like many European clubs, FC St. Pauli football is part of a larger umbrella organization that also promotes teams in rugby, baseball, bowling, roller derby, chess, handball, cycling, skittles, softball and table tennis. For practitioners seeking economies of scale, you'll find the same dynamic in Barcelona, where the world-renowned football club (starring Lionel Messi) is part of a sports conglomerate fielding clubs in basketball, ice hockey, roller hockey and rugby.

So why tell you about a run-of-the-mill, second-tier team playing in the shadows of Bundesliga? This is no runt-of-the-litter pup. St. Pauli sells out nearly every game and averages more than 28,000 spectators a game. And although the club dropped to the third German division in the early 2000s, it has a devoted fan base that prides itself on being truly against racism, homophobia and sexism. Interestingly, this pro-diversity fan culture has led the team to expand its stadium, thus selling more tickets and driving merchandise sales of pirate skull-themed T-shirts, hats, shot glasses, beer mugs and ash trays.

We're telling you about FC St. Pauli because, as we hinted above, its "secret sauce" is how it welcomes every under-represented segment from the diverse Hamburg culture to its fan base with open arms: straight, gay, smokers, bikers, cross-dressers, the poor, transsexuals, men, women, immigrants, tourists, ex-pats, and more. In other words, the human zoo. Each and every human. All religious and political affiliations as well as those who have no interest in either.

That struck us as being distinctly different from what we see in most major college and professional stadiums in North America, where seat pricing has driven anyone in the margins out of the building and marketing approaches, although open in content, normally target particular segments or markets.

There are numerous articles in academic sports management literature that describe the racial, gender and cultural biases that exist in our fan bases. Short term, a focus on revenue generation may be OK, but long term, given the rapidly changing makeup and composition of our population, we must evolve to strategies built on diversity and understanding of differences. Currently, although statistics on the diversity breakdowns of the average attendee at sporting events are hard to come by and are of limited accuracy, observation at most North American venues is a whiter and richer crowd than the general population or larger fan base for most clubs.

Given the lack of public data, we reached out to AJ Maestas, CEO of Navigate Research, who noted that in a recent study for an NBA franchise, the fan demographics showed notably strong diversity. Nearly half of fans were women. But we guess few might arrive at that conclusion based on the proliferation of male-focused media, predominantly male fantasy leagues and straight, white male–dominated administrations.

This leads to the question: Can a pro-diversity approach work in North America like it does for FC St. Pauli?

We think so, but we decided to check with a professional to see if diversity and inclusion is on the minds of those in the trenches. Jason Smorol, general manager of the International League's Syracuse Chiefs, told us, "From day one, we have been about inclusion. Exclusion makes no sense. We believe that our product is affordable, family fun, and that is a universal concept. Why would we not want to market our product available to 100 percent of our market? That's why we have Little League Night, Cancer Awareness Night, Military Appreciation Night and Jackie Robinson Tribute Night."

Even Hollywood is recognizing this trend in movies like the *Fast and the Furious* franchise, which features a wide range of distinct ethnicities. As the *New York Times* wrote in its review of the latest movie, "'Furious 7' extends its predecessors' inclusive, stereotype-resistant ethic. Compared to almost any other large-scale, big-studio enterprise, the 'Furious' brand practices a slick, no-big-deal multiculturalism, and nods to both feminism and domestic traditionalism."

So, for all of you out there—and there are many—who are working hard to grow your professional or collegiate teams, your club events, your facilities, sports properties and brands . . . take a page from the book of a small German football club and try opening your doors a little wider.

It'll be good for business and for society, too.

40

Second-Tier Events, Health Initiatives Will Gain Foothold in 2015

Published February 2, 2015

WITH 2014 NOW WELL BEHIND US, we spent some time thinking about "skating to where the puck is going." That is, to play the role of futurists and, in taking a page out of Wayne Gretzky's book, telling our friends and industry associates what we think are a couple of exciting prospects for 2015. So, what should a sports entrepreneur look for in 2015 and beyond?

For starters, we think you'll be reading a lot more about the growth of second-tier international games and championships, those events that once were relegated to small cities or locations where the specific sport was played. We're thinking specifically of Canada, where the June–July FIFA Women's World Cup (held in seven cities) will be followed by the Pan Am and Parapan Am Games in Toronto. And the evidence doesn't stop there. For instance, the NHL recently announced the return of the World Cup of Hockey (slated for Toronto as well in 2016). And a new flagship national team baseball event, the Premier 12 world championship, will launch in Taiwan and Japan in November under the direction of the World Baseball Softball Confederation.

The enhanced value of live sports television in today's digital environment is going to drive interest in these less than mega-events as more sports networks have more slots for content and remain desperate for the live content that continues to attract viewers and streamers.

Unlike years past, these "other" games will garner greater attention, including:

The interest of top conferences. The Canadian Sponsorship Forum is linking up with the FIFA Women's World Cup in Edmonton, and the Toronto Pan American Economic Summit will be held on the eve of the Pan Am Games.

Bigger sponsors. The 2015 Pan Am and Parapan Am Games include a sponsor roster of CIBC, Atos, Chevrolet, Cisco, Live Nation and Cirque du Soleil.

Greater media coverage. NBC covered a record 52 hours of the Paralympic Games in 2014.

There is still interest in the biggest global mega-events. Witness the level of competition Boston faces to potentially host the 2024 Summer Olympic Games. We say potentially because, despite receiving the U.S. Olympic Committee's approval, Boston will still have to beat global cities like Paris, Rome, Berlin (or Hamburg), Melbourne (or Brisbane), Istanbul, and either Durban or Johannesburg in South Africa. No easy feat, as many bid cities—including the aforementioned Toronto and Paris—can attest.

Our second forecast for the near future is related to the other side of sports—participation sports and the benefits that our passion can provide to society. Largely neglected relative to health outcomes, the role and commitment of big sports in a healthier society is gaining traction, and interest will increase considerably in the coming years. Specifically, we sense that a new era of sports is coming.

But hear this clearly: It is not about spectatorship or entertainment. It involves the true coronation of health.

In most developed countries, only a scant few do enough physical activity to curb the tide of inactivity-based diseases. In North America, a mere fraction of youth and adults do enough activity to keep their bodies strong and healthy. The marketing potential and opportunities to engage foreign governments, charitable foundations, health-focused national governing bodies, sports federations and the not-for-profit sector are high.

Despite the power of sports as entertainment, we believe that sports leaders will begin stepping up and identifying beneficial margins from our increasingly inactive and obese world. Sports has a role to play, one that can both help the society in which we plan and increase the credibility of our field broadly.

Physical activity and regular exercise work for some, but the social, team-building and competitive power of sports has a major role to play to get more of us active—not just North Americans and not just kids. Adults are increasingly sedentary, with studies showing fewer than 20 percent of us do enough and 40 percent of us are overweight. These declining rates also have long-term implications for the sports business, as fewer participants could lead to fewer fans, fewer spectators, fewer viewers and lower revenue.

We'd be remiss without noting that many of the sports leagues, federations and clubs have a similar view to ours on this double benefit of helping society while simultaneously helping influence their own futures. Think about the NFL's Play 60, MLB's Urban Youth Academy (with its Pitch, Hit and Run program), NBA Fit and the NHL's Hockey Is for Everyone. On top of this are the efforts of NGBs and nonprofit sports organizations.

But are we as an industry doing enough? Probably not. But no group will fly this healthy-living banner unless they see others sharing the load. And few will invest without seeing clear linkage to future sustainable earnings. It's a nice catch-22.

From a research standpoint, we know a passion for sports can be inspired in a number of ways, from attending a special game with a parent or guardian, watching a spectacular performance on television or learning to love a game after some form of regular play.

It is the last of these that is coming under threat for many of us. So, for the larger benefit (society's health) and a self-serving one (your organization's ROI), please plan to put some regular sports participation on the calendar for you and yours in 2015 and beyond.

41

This Industry Could Learn Something from Scholars

Published October 13, 2014

ON OCT. 24 IN PHILADELPHIA, Syracuse University professor and graduate program director Chad McEvoy will receive one of the most prestigious academic awards for a sports management scholar. The award is the Sport Marketing Association's 2014 Sutton Award, which recognizes a sport marketing professor who has made a difference in our wide-reaching industry.

As winner, McEvoy will be recognized for a career of practitioner and academic excellence that has incorporated a relevant doctoral thesis, consistent scholarly publication, authorship of two textbooks, editorship of two journals, industry consulting and legal testimony.

When we learned of his selection, we wondered whether enough sports industry executives knew who McEvoy was or, for that matter, who any of the world's leading sports management scholars were. It's an interesting question because our sense is that while McEvoy has spent considerable time focusing on revenue generation in spectator sports (following a career in the industry working in marketing and fund-raising for two Division I Football Bowl Subdivision athletic departments), his profession as an educator might suggest to some

9. An overhead shot of the Carrier Dome during a Syracuse men's basketball game. *Courtesy of Syracuse University Athletics.*

practitioners that his efforts are dated or out of touch with the realities of sports' daily challenges. Funny that.

You see, McEvoy is one of a few dozen star professors in our field who are both thought leaders and highly engaged in industry. Academicians like the namesake of McEvoy's award, Bill Sutton at South Florida, Jim Kahler and Heather Lawrence-Benedict in Ohio University's world-ranked program, Simon Chadwick at Coventry (U.K.), Matt Robinson (Delaware), Bettina Cornwell (Oregon), George Foster (Stanford), Glenn Wong (UMass) and Ken Shropshire (Pennsylvania) publish and educate in the belief that their work matters to the sports industry and is relevant to its current and future executives.

Like his peers, McEvoy bridges academia and industry often. For example, McEvoy currently teaches a class that is essentially a working pipeline for the New York Yankees ticket sales department.

In the academic world, at conferences like those hosted by SMA or the North American Society of Sport Management or the University of South Carolina's Sport Entertainment and Venues Tomorrow conference, top scholars are widely recognized, and their opinions are sought by many scholars. These individuals are often asked to participate in blue-chip consulting projects, as experts in legal cases and in major commissions that influence the trajectory of sports as an industry.

For example, in 2008, the Knight Commission on Intercollegiate Athletics asked McEvoy to serve as a panelist and share his research on the effectiveness of NCAA penalties. In 2013, McEvoy led a think tank with top athletic directors and senior college athletic administrators at the National Association of Collegiate Directors of Athletics convention with an aim for using research to provide data-based solutions to challenges facing the billion-dollar intercollegiate athletics business. McEvoy's research has touched on crucial industry issues such as pricing effectiveness, sponsorship effectiveness and the impact of college athletic success for universities. That's no small set of agendas.

The point of this isn't that any professor knows all or can fix any problem. They can't. But it does make us wonder how many other professors are out there who should be providing more statistical and educated input on how to solve the numerous challenges facing our industry. The reality, though, is that in many cases, the sports industry does not hold the academy in high regard.

This needs to change. Many elite academicians and leading programs have suggested to us that we're not there yet. Not like other business disciplines such as accounting, finance and management. So, what gives?

Want to talk about sponsorship losing its flavor? Concussion (in all sports) changing the trajectory of professional competition? Sleep patterns dictating performance? Revenue streams not keeping up? Globalization? Digital technology's impact on fan attendance? Sophistication in the secondary ticket market? Economic rates of success for in-stadium promotions? Video games and fantasy league influence on attendance?

We know well that sports management and marketing scholars are poring over our industry's facts and producing legitimate findings that our industry should see. Trouble is, if someone isn't working in the industry, they might be picking up a stigma. What we've generally heard is this: "If you were any good, you'd be working in the industry. Not teaching."

Such a sentiment suggests that only industry professionals can know what is going on. If that's true, we've become an inbred, closed society that will struggle to keep up with the fastest moving of industry sectors. It also means we've turned our back on teachers who might play a huge role in helping sports businesses solve their future problems in large part by shaping and supplying their future leaders.

42

CrossFit Shows Strength to Excel among Participatory Sports

Published August 11, 2014

WE WATCHED WITH INTEREST recently as the Reebok CrossFit Games were televised on ESPN. Like most sports industry practitioners, we'd heard about this event and probably thought it was a nice way for young people to show off their muscles. Was this a fad that would pop up, catch a bit of attention and then just fade away?

In chatting about it, we thought this was likely another participatory rage to put up on the shelf with karate in the '70s, racquetball in the '80s, yoga in the '90s, and Pilates, P90X and Zumba aerobics more recently. Somewhere, we thought, a minor celebrity was lying on a beach, pocketing a mint after inventing the latest way to fight obesity and flabbiness.

But after seeing CrossFit live (and checking out its website and chatting with a few friends, students and colleagues who participate), our views changed substantially, if not completely. Like the Tough Mudder, Warrior Dash, Spartan Race and Ironman events of the world (all of which have taken their share of the sport-participation pie), CrossFit looks poised to follow in notable tracks and perhaps go beyond.

Looking for an unlikely game-changing industry example? How about the Ultimate Fighting Championship? That's what CrossFit may be. In the same way UFC and mixed martial arts allow participants from any fighting background to participate (but also expand their fighting techniques), the CrossFit Games test athletes who don't always know their specific events until just before they compete, and they draw from a variety of workout disciplines that incorporate wide-ranging fitness exercises and expertise.

So imagine needing to be able to do not only 125 pull-ups, but also swimming, running, climbing, jumping, any Olympic-style lifting and more. It's truly a test of all-around fitness with a strong dose of strategy thrown in. Anyone who watches, who has any kind of athletic background, is likely to observe at least one discipline in which they could shine.

"CrossFit works because it tests the 10 general physical skills. It doesn't strive to be great at just one particular skill; it wants everyone to be good at everything," said Lance Weber, a trainer at CrossFit Billings in Montana. "It's a sport that can test the elite athletes of all sports and fitness competitions alike, as well as be 100 percent scalable for older generations as well as any athlete in between."

So why is CrossFit a hot topic? Well, one reason may be the movement away from NCAA-style regulations and the disengagement of "regular" athletes. Another could be the culture.

"The camaraderie in CrossFit is amazing," said Weber, whose facility is owned by Kerry and Yurii Hanson of Billings. "It's the one place where you will see the winners turning back to cheer on their competition. To be honest, the people in last place are getting the loudest cheers and applause, whether it's in the gym or at the games."

That's much, we imagine, like watching the final finishers of the Ironman crossing the finish line before midnight. It's in those settings that the "every finisher is a winner" motto shows its value.

"I played baseball in high school, dreaming of going to the pros," Weber said. "But competing at a level of such high caliber wasn't in the cards for me. I came across CrossFit in college and found a new sport that was more challenging than I could imagine. People from all over the world were getting the opportunity to become elite competitive athletes or else really reaching lifetime fitness goals. Either way, you've got to admit, that beats sweating on a treadmill for hours."

Heather Lawrence, a professor of sport management at Ohio University and a CrossFit Level 1 trainer, said there seems to be some misunderstanding about CrossFit. "[It] often gets viewed as an elite club of superior athletes pushing themselves to the brink of exhaustion during every workout," Lawrence said. "In reality, coaches modify workouts for each individual to ensure the workout is high intensity but meets the individual's needs. So it's not uncommon for CrossFit classes to include a teenage girl living with cystic fibrosis, a stay-at-home mother, former college student athletes, weekend warriors and a few high-level athletes all completing the workout together with modifications as needed. The result is a welcoming community of people bonding through the shared experience of pushing their physical and mental limits."

As people of all ages in developed countries battle the inactivity crisis in a world with numerous attractive inactive pursuits from spectatorship to video games on iPads, properties that are cool and sexy may just be the secret to helping stem health consequences and spiraling health care costs. And although we often talk about youth stagnation, we know adults need fun active programming as well. CrossFit's growth trajectory may suggest older folks are figuring that out.

That ESPN carried the 2014 Reebok CrossFit Games last month on all of its platforms (ESPN, ESPN2, WatchESPN and primarily ESPN3) and Reebok is leveraging a 10-year partnership with CrossFit (including naming rights) should count for something. Reebok and ESPN3 may seem like lesser lights to some industry veterans, but give CrossFit credit for cementing these deals.

As for us, while we're still not 100 percent sure about this latest fitness movement, we are certain CrossFit, Tough Mudder and the UFC should show up on the radars of industry practitioners. In the case of participation sports, get a handle on what makes something fun, sexy and cool (at the same time). For those with many constituent institutions (think the NCAA), give your "body" a chance to let more student athletes shine, particularly female athletes.

43

The Growing, Changing Nature of Sports Management Instruction

Published December 16, 2013

ONE OF US was in Surfers Paradise, Australia, recently and met with a professor of surfing from a very reputable university. His academic purview was not built around teaching college students how to surf but rather how to manage the business nuances of the surfing industry and delivering it to the next sustainable level.

Naturally, we both zoomed back in time in our minds—to the age of 18 or 19—and imagined how cool it would be to tell friends and parents that we were majoring in surfing and actually getting a degree for it.

But it also made us wonder about the number of sports marketing/management programs around the world and whether they are all selling similar variations on the same myth. That is: offering young, fanatical (about sports) and idealistic folks (many who lack focus and a true understanding of how competitive the sports industry is) the chance to imagine they could work amid the flash and glamour of the "big show."

We would start by warning them that an entry-level job in sports may offer only a $25,000 salary, that hundreds will apply for entry-level jobs and that without a connection to the hiring party, they will probably lose out. It's a competitive ocean out there, and a sports management or sports marketing degree is no guarantee of career success, especially if the individual's skill set is drawn from a vague set of courses providing little specificity.

In fact, one of us recently spoke to a friend who applied for the executive directorship of a state-level sports organization, and he came in second . . . out of 250 head-hunted candidates. But the reason why people "chase the dream" and start at $25,000 is that they hear of people hitting six-figure salaries quickly and thus believe they can achieve the same outcome.

Can college sports management programs offer that to all of their enrolled students? Optimistic answer? Maybe. Simple answer? No.

But we do believe that well-constructed sports management programs and top-line employee training programs will continue to allow young, well-educated, highly motivated former students to get in the game. Indeed, one of our former students was just named the lead on a major international world championship event that drives multimillion-person TV audiences and eight-figure profit margins. All that in less than 10 years out of university.

How did he do it? He was diligent—ever since his first year—and focused. He followed his passion, built his network through legitimate relationships, paid his dues, sought out unique experiences and did this all while honing specialized skills and knowledge. It was a no-brainer hiring him for the job. So, what are we really saying?

The sport business is complex like other industries. The cream rises to the top. Long-term planning and career development actually matter. Many want in, but few make the cut. Many are ultimately seduced by more money in less glamorous jobs. Many go back to the traditional trades. And, others, bless their hearts, only want to work 35 hours a week instead of 70.

But what's next? Majoring in the NFL? Professional sports ticketing as a minor? Sport marketing with a specialization in NBA sponsors? Yes, yes and yes. That specificity is coming.

But on top of that, there's a big game-changer approaching. It's one where top professors or industry professionals are provided incentives to teach classes online. This emerging process is called MOOCs (massive open online courses), and it's a slow-bubbling rage in the higher-education business. We know a lot about them because one of us recently filmed seven video segments to be shown once per week for seven weeks. The course launched Oct. 14 and is available to anyone anywhere to view anytime. For now, this course is free, but futurists suggest students will soon pay for great classes because they don't want teaching assistants who have never been in the real world teaching a class at 8:00 a.m. on Mondays.

This new generation of students, raised in part on video games and fantasy sports leagues, will program their own pleasure and take world-class professors at 2:00 in the morning. Digital technology allows that, and as great professors are identified, they'll be encouraged to record their lectures and allow university systems to sell their content in perpetuity much the way iTunes sells historic "classical" music made by the Stones or Rush.

One challenge to this model is that students will lose the ability to personally interact with their professor and discuss random topics before or after class. In the digital university, the student might never get out of bed and, at best, periodically Skype with the professor or join chat room discussions that make students feel like they're in private viewing rooms with their professor but unable to interrupt to ask an immediate question.

We won't debate the evolution of pedagogy here, but suffice to say, MOOCs will become increasingly popular because they'll provide a greater sense of control for the student. The capitalism of efficient, well-designed courses taught by interesting, entertaining professors will eclipse (in some settings) the requirement of taking a "bad" class from a weak professor. That universities have always enjoyed a monopoly with their enrolled students will, logically, come under attack. And trust us, the inefficient, overpriced product or service will struggle to survive.

But we also predict sport management (as a field of study) will continue growing because these days the "circus" never leaves town and the content is still dynamic.

44

How to Spot, Benefit from Next Disruptive Innovation in Sports

Published November 4, 2013

HERE'S THE SCENARIO: You're stuck in an airport, and out of sheer boredom you wander into the concourse bookstore to consider a reading purchase. Suddenly, you notice an abundance of business books related to technology's impact on business, management and leadership. Logical, right?

But maybe that's just the beginning. Maybe you're supposed to be wondering about the process of disruptive technology in sports. Are you ready for the pending convergence of television, Internet, radio and voice into one device? Are you considering what impending development might next change the dynamics of your sport, like aero lightweight frames in cycling? What about forecasting those unexpected new markets, like the thousands now competing in Warrior, Spartan, Tough Mudder and, our new favorite, "zombie" runs?

Our attention was piqued about a year ago in Australia. It started with a line of research with two academic colleagues (Ann Pegoraro of Laurentian University's School of Sports Administration and Nadège Levallet at Queen's University's School of Business) on "disruptive innovation." By definition, that phrase includes any change or evolution that has more than an expected change on the industry. From a scholarly standpoint, we are seeking to model these innovations and then try to arm practitioners with a framework by which to forecast their arrival and navigate their reality.

That sounds attractive, but practically it's tricky. Things that are disruptive often are resisted, and in the following examples you may see what really happens when disruption occurs.

If we go back in time, we can talk about athletic concepts like the development of titanium drivers in golf or curved sticks in ice hockey. These were product innovations that changed the game. But let's look at how the game was managed. What did Danny Biasone's 24-second clock do to professional basketball? How did Title IX change the dynamics of the NCAA? How did Billy Beane's "Moneyball" approach influence the data-mining revolution in team sports?

There are others we could cite, such as the American League adding a designated-hitter rule or various leagues instituting salary caps, granting free agency or establishing player drafts to foster or ensure league parity. We could go down the safety route as well and talk about devices like pop-up vents on race cars (to keep them from flying into the crowd) or the NHL's recent mandate to include visors as mandatory wear.

At the venue level, we could discuss personal seat licenses, the creation of luxury boxes at stadiums or the advent of electronic tickets to replace paper ducats.

We could go on, as you could, with examples that were very disruptive or were just a logical progression of technology that was expected or overdue. Indeed, the list in this run of examples would be almost endless since sports has required numerous innovations to keep games and races safe, exciting and sustainable.

But here's a key thought for you: In the technology world, discussions on innovation and disruption are as regular as nightly scores and player updates. That means the key in this discussion is helping owners, management and sports marketers spot disruptive opportunities before they arrive and then help them to adapt or make them happen. After that, someone, usually a commissioner or a series operator, needs to deal with them.

This leads to a series of questions:

• Have you heard about material printing, where scientists are now able to print golf clubs, running shoes and other sports equipment on demand? The potential to disrupt the entire manufacturing process is already there. It may be many years away or perhaps is already racing at us.

• Are you regularly scanning blogs and industry reports for new developments?

• Are you staying in touch with that wise old professor of yours to see what he or she is observing?

• Do you really understand what the process of disruptive change is and how much more to expect in the future?

We're early in the research process, but two steps are critical. First, practitioners in club management, marketing agencies and corporate sponsors all need human resources at their organizations who are in the know and constantly watching for disruptive clues as they occur. This means these "forecasters" are researching their industry (or segment) and all the elements that could disrupt it. More than likely, these folks are doing Web research, following scientific journals, attending key conferences and informing their colleagues that something unusual is happening.

For example, in 1989, if cyclist Laurent Fignon had employed a coach or adviser who understood aerodynamics and new equipment, he could have adopted the new technology like Greg LeMond did and, in turn, possibly have captured his third Tour de France (as opposed to finishing second).

Second, someone at the organization has to respond when the alarm is sounded and include these potential disruptions in the annual planning process. This, we know, is easier said than done. But look at Silicon Valley and tech startups: They deal with this hourly.

We think this is an annual consideration (or should be) and that numerous agents inside the organization need to be ready with resources in place. That's easy to suggest when you are camped out in the ivory tower as we are or pushing others in the communal think tank. But the rate of change, particularly in technology, is quicker than you think. Logically, it must be almost as fast in sports since our industry relies on technology to keep the fans and consumers buying our respective products and services.

Remember: Evolution rewards those who adapt the fastest and most efficiently.

45

When Goliath Doesn't Win—and Why

Published February 13, 2012

FORBES ON NOV. 30 released its annual financial ranking of NHL teams. Although there's debate about the accuracy and validity of some of the numbers, most who analyze the data believe that by using the same methodology over time, the relative differences between teams and the collective longitudinal changes they face are reasonable when making club-purchase assessments or for discussing research focusing on real revenues and profitability.

One item in the report that got our attention was the team whose worth increased proportionally the most over the previous year: the reborn Winnipeg Jets. Why are the Jets worth more in Winnipeg than playing as the Thrashers in Atlanta?

Our take? When talking about ticket buyers, fan avidity is sometimes more important than quantity. The return of the Jets to Manitoba's capital is particularly notable when you recall that 16 years ago (in 1996) the club left town ownerless and virtually unable to compete in the NHL. Then, before last season, True North Sports and Entertainment purchased the Thrashers for $110 million and paid a $60 million relocation fee to the league. Now the club is worth $164 million, a 21 percent increase from *Forbes*'s estimate the previous year.

The Jets followed up their move with a well-designed ticket-pricing model, a smart rebrand, the construction of a shrewd management team and the presentation of a sound business model. Now, this all may sound like a good case study for students, but one thing is important to question: How could a club increase in value by 21 percent in moving from Atlanta to Winnipeg?

Some numbers to ponder: Atlanta represents the 10th largest metropolis in North America (5.3 million people), is one of the nation's top media markets and is home to numerous other professional sports teams. Winnipeg features a population of less than 700,000, is one of the smallest cities for a professional sports team in Canada (or the U.S.) and offers limited media presence.

But maybe something is afoot in pro sports. Green Bay dominated the recent NFL regular season, Oklahoma City is an emerging NBA power, and Milwaukee and St. Louis played for MLB's National League championship last October.

Is it possible that small markets can survive and thrive in big-time sports? The answer is no, or, best case, it's highly unlikely. Any MBA student will tell you that economies of scale (and the presence of Fortune 500 sponsors) dictate most commercial outcomes. Still, it wouldn't surprise us to see an NHL team move to Quebec City (whose population equals Winnipeg's) or for the NFL to want teams in Buffalo and New Orleans despite needing a quality team in Los Angeles.

The reason? Small-market teams, with their grassroots marketing and sense of community ownership, often feature more avidity than their city-mouse cousins. Plus, most mega-markets have multiple teams fighting for fan attention.

Further, the presence of Davids fighting Goliaths gives off a different perception to the media and fans when the word "parity" is thrown around by league commissioners. Indeed, collective-bargaining agreements now routinely attempt to provide environments in which smaller-market teams can compete financially.

On another continent, Manchester, England, should not be the seat of power in English football . . . but it is. That's why it's vital for

North American leagues to value their tiny markets and protect them from the very challenges their smaller populations create. If every team is London, New York or Toronto, it's much harder to sell an underdog.

That's why when Buffalo goes to four straight Super Bowls or Milwaukee makes the NL Championship Series, the health of a pro sport (both in asset appreciation for owners and in appreciation by fans) goes up broadly.

In politics, they say New York and Los Angeles (or Toronto and Vancouver) select the candidates, but everyone knows it's the smaller markets in between that elect the president (or prime minister). Perhaps a parallel exists in sports.

46

Sports Industry Must Find Moral Courage to Act amid Crisis

Published January 2, 2012

HAVE YOU EVER HAD AN EMPLOYEE, a co-worker or friend come to you and admit they've attempted suicide? That they are depressed and their marriage is falling apart? That they've been embezzling? That they've been gambling money that they shouldn't have? That they're having an affair with a junior employee or intern? That they can't stand working for or with another employee?

Our guess is that many of you have found yourself in that situation, but, unlike the matters still smoldering at Penn State, Syracuse and elsewhere, you've thought the best course of action was to keep your mouth shut. People know how to get counseling if they need it. People should keep their noses out of other people's business. The person confiding in me doesn't see me as an authority figure, they just need someone to talk to that they can trust. They confided in me and expect me to keep this confidential. Ahh, you'll get over that . . . or even . . . I've got your back, buddy. Any of those lines sound familiar?

In light of unspeakable allegations at Penn State and the current situation at Syracuse, the spotlight on responsibility, on moral obligation, on ethical values is suddenly shining brightly on millions in the sports industry. Most of us think we'll still be able to sidestep any great commitment to justice or intervention (or equality for that matter), but the truth is that these situations are likely to serve as a great historic line in the sand. The attention drawn to these issues, by those inside and outside of sport, has been unprecedented.

From November 2011 onward, the media, fans, members of your family, your partner, your children and friends are going to be able to say, "Why didn't you do more?" And to cop a plea, that you told your supervisor, is probably not going to cut it. From today on, people will expect that if you saw something and didn't commit to righting a wrong or to speaking up, you were "soft" and in some places/cases you should be removed from your position. These new expectations will certainly be enhanced if you hold a position of any public stature, like the coach or athletic director of an NCAA program or a similar role with a professional team.

Now, hold on, you're probably saying. We can't turn the sports industry into some Orwellian Big Brother machine. We can't become the modern-day equivalent of the East German Stasi, with informants lurking behind every wall or ceiling. We mustn't overreact. In fact, you might be suggesting, we're obligated to wait until all the facts in the Penn State and Syracuse cases are verified.

No, we're not. We need to better acknowledge some innate human tendencies as well as the importance of basic (but comprehensive) moral obligations. For all of us, this is more important than the case at hand, but let's be clear: The case at hand has drawn the needed attention for the argument to be heard. And attention to victims—people we need to care deeply about—everywhere.

Marquette University marketing professor Gene Laczniak sees it this way: "When we see abuses or troubles, the easiest thing to do is nothing. So, when faced with some potential intervention to help, whether to connect someone needing a jump-start for their car or to delay our journey to give witness or aid after an accident, there is a natural human disposition not to get involved. Someone else's problem, we rationalize, will likely sort itself out in due time."

Laczniak has spent much of his academic career writing about ethics and building knowledge in this area. It is interesting when he says, "Applied ethics would suggest a higher duty in the case of too many opt-outs. There are times, especially when an action can stop or prevent grave harm to others, when we must summon the moral courage to act decisively. Various philosophers have enumerated self-evident duties (at least self-evident to reflective thinkers) to render assistance when we are opportunistically able. Such moral courage is necessary both to affirm our humanity and to contribute to a better community."

Laczniak's views inspire a number of interesting and thought-provoking questions:

• Would Major League Baseball have been better off if trainers or team physicians had reported suspicions or knowledge of steroid usage?

• Would college sports and the NCAA hold a stronger reputation if university presidents prohibited booster gifts from being earmarked for their athletics programs?

• Should NFL or CFL coaches and owners insist their players be tested for synthetic human growth hormones in hopes of preventing a future scandal and leveling the playing field?

• What would've happened if everyone involved with the Tour de France, particularly the sponsors, had said "enough is enough" when Tour champions were routinely found guilty of doping?

The tragedies at Penn State and Syracuse provide a teaching moment with the upside of forcing all of us to rethink the ethical duties each of us has to help nurture the human solidarity that affirms the goodness of competitive sport. But what should we be telling our peers and employees? In business schools and sport management programs, curriculums include much on issues related to ethics, crisis management and risk management, all elements that—if applied practically—would lead to the consideration of tough questions like those listed above.

Why, then, do we continue to prioritize short-term reputations and loyalty over the long-term best interests and the right thing? We bring this question forward today, in the midst of the media scrutiny, to push our industry—practitioners and educators alike—to make ethics important, to do more than talk about risk, to take a prevention focus to crises. Simply put, we all need to do more.

47

Gender Equity Best Served by Creativity, Not Loopholes

Published July 18, 2011

WE NOTED WITH INTEREST a recent front-page column in the *New York Times* about numerous NCAA universities and colleges "relying on deception" to "undermine gender equity." You saw that story, right? Even if you didn't, it's worth noting that one of the world's leading publications allotted front-page space to this topic.

Is it a good thing? As two fathers with daughters, we absolutely think so because gender equity is of huge interest to us personally as well as professionally.

The article uncovered numerous examples of schools employing shady practices to get around the concept of 1-to-1 participation between men and women. The story noted that vaunted schools such as Cornell, Duke and Texas A&M have used male practice players for female teams because those men count as women under federal accounting rules. In some places, that's called a convenient loophole.

Evidently, schools such as Marshall could count unqualified athletes (those not good enough to practice against scholarship athletes) to round out female team rosters. The worst situation may have involved the University of South Florida, a Big East school, which seemingly was exposed for having certified seventy-five female runners on its women's cross-country team in order to help USF comply with Title IX.

Wait a minute. What's going on here? We're approaching the 40th anniversary of Title IX, and schools are double- and triple-counting women to get around the fact they don't have true gender equity? That's more than concerning. It's illegal.

And, most importantly, legal or not, what does this mean for female athletes? Are we lying to our daughters when we tell them Title IX and CIS's Equity and Equality Policy (CIS: Canadian Interuniversity Sport—Canada's NCAA equivalent) provide them with the same opportunities as their brothers?

The problem seems to fester in the reality, sometimes mouthed by athletic directors at major institutions, that it's easier to add student athletes to a Division I roster than to start a new sport. But we'd like to ask if that truism is always true. Or, is the problem based on which sports can generate revenue and which ones will lose a boatload? Are we afraid to invent new sports or find creative solutions?

There's no questioning that the availability of finite resources (travel budgets, facilities, coaching, equipment, etc.) makes it easier to avoid adding new sports, but—as we often tell our students—there are always other ways. Management is, at its core, a creative as well as a quantitative science.

The recent rescue of the about-to-be-cut women's hockey team at St. Mary's University in Halifax is a prime example. Following an outcry when the team was put on the chopping block by the university, donations (led by Canadian Tire, a Canadian retail institution) saved the team—and a positive, far-reaching story for the sport, the university and Canadian Tire emerged. The term "entrepreneurial" comes to mind in looking at this case and prompts the question: Where are the true entrepreneurs for sports?

The crux of the quota dilemma, often bemoaned by those responsible for achieving gender equity, is that men's football—the bear that usually drives the majority of revenue (but not necessarily profits) for a university—requires 60 to 100 young men. Given North America's historical love of this game, finding those young men and filling a team with 22 starters is not difficult. But finding a new sport that could easily attract 60 to 100 women is much harder because of the on-field/court/ice player limitations of many traditional sports like lacrosse (10), softball (nine), ice hockey (six,) and basketball (five).

But what if a new sport were invented that combined the game flow of soccer, basketball and lacrosse with the ability to generate true 60-person rosters?

Want an idea? Look to other countries and cultures. Take Australia, for example. The Aussies' biggest sport is Australian Rules Football, and the game is played with no pads (hence reduced cost) on a large oval pitch. Traditionally, teams have 22 players (18 on the field at once with four interchanges), but it is easy to imagine large rosters with frequent substitutions. It's feasible to imagine bringing this model to our existing football or soccer stadiums.

If Aussie Rules is too far afield for you, then think of a special sport or adapted sport (like Ultimate Frisbee) that is attractive to young athletes, interesting to university student spectators, yet could be good for TV and online streaming. Other industries do it every day (adapt/create products), so why can't we?

As a side note, one of us is from Springfield, Mass., and few children grow up there without knowing that Dr. James Naismith, a Canadian, invented the game of basketball in order to create an indoor sport during the winter. This was more than 100 years ago and is still talked about widely today. Have we lost the ability to invent or modify? Maybe so.

But this truism remains: If we want gender equity, we've got to stop focusing on dated concepts and loopholes and look for creative ways to make the word "equal" exciting and not limiting.

48

The Secrets of Leadership Are Often Found at the Bottom

Published June 6, 2011

IN OUR EXPERIENCES teaching students aspiring to serve as future managers in the sports industry, we've noted a growing curiosity about North America's sports executives. Indeed, both of us frequently create leadership exercises, and one of us even designed an open-ended case assignment for an undergraduate sport management class at Syracuse that went like this:

Selecting from league commissioners Roger Goodell (NFL), David Stern (NBA), Gary Bettman (NHL) and media chiefs George Bodenheimer (ESPN) and Brian Roberts (Comcast), write a five-page analysis of where the selected individual came from (examining the trajectory of his career) and describe what early leadership traits (or experiences) best explain his approach to managing his multibillion-dollar enterprise.

What emerged was a hodgepodge of superficial descriptions detailing recent high-profile challenges the above individuals faced. Much seemed missing. Only one paper on Goodell started as far back as his sporting career in high school. Only one enterprising student dug deep enough to write about Stern working at his family's deli during summers in law school. Only a few included the nugget that

Bodenheimer started in ESPN's mailroom. None ventured a guess on what these men learned at the beginning of their careers, how their career ambitions were nurtured or how they developed the requisite skills to successfully steward high-profile organizations.

Granted, taking students to task for writing bad "book reports" is easy, but at the core of this challenge is a reality that teaching sports leadership development (as opposed to regurgitating statements of accomplishment) is often a difficult meal to serve.

Averting a lockout (or forcing one) is certainly part of the territory that goes with running a league. As is keeping 30 or more owners satisfied with your work. Similarly, buying expensive broadcast rights or acquiring a major media property (as in the case of Comcast taking a 51 percent position with NBCUniversal) is complicated and requires enormous stamina, delegation, instinct and decisiveness.

But how should today's students think about the nuances of leadership and the development of managerial fluidity? As a generation, they're often seen as overly entitled and have been led by their parents to believe they are wonderful, brilliant and deserving of better than whatever they've been offered or given.

These baby boomer spawn arrived courtesy of history's most successful generation. Yet many may not attain the same levels of success in their lifetime as their parents. And that covers not only financial accomplishment but also health, longevity and happiness.

We believe strongly that a disconnect exists between parents' excessive coddling and their children's ability to learn valuable leadership traits. It may be parents' right to assist their child, but keeping a young person from starting at the bottom may alter his or her capacity to master group dynamics and truly seek out servant-leadership moments on thankless tasks. This problem manifests itself when these same children graduate from college expecting to lead departments or divisions less than 90 days after graduating. Trust us, this is a major challenge facing higher education today, and not just in North America.

For some, it may be hard to believe, but here's a hard truth: Entitlement without hard work is a recipe for disaster. Leaders like those mentioned have faced decades of leadership development where traits like integrity, inclusion and imagination were honed during career-defining "fires." In each case, though, these leaders must have drawn on early-career lessons that allowed them to solve problems and take on new ones.

In a recent trip to New York City, one of us had the chance to sit down with Bettman and discuss the realities facing his league. Based on an hour-long discussion on many topics, it became evident that, first, this man is very intelligent and well-versed on all things legal, sponsorship-related, consumer mass marketing, player welfare, social media and so on.

Second, it was obvious Bettman has a firm grasp of what is happening at all levels of his sport. We had deep discussions on issues ranging from youth participation in ice hockey, equipment costs for families, sponsorship evaluation, player injuries and Sochi 2014.

Finally, and perhaps most importantly, it's worth noting the clarity of Bettman's focus when it came to listening to his owners. In this regard, like any smart manager, it was evident that he understands that leadership is about making sure you have the right vision and the expertise required to achieve that vision. Perhaps no better proof may exist than observing that the NHL's business model (at the moment) appears to be working for the majority of teams.

So what's the link between uncertain expectations for our graduating students and the shrewdness of long-term leaders in sport? First, given the low turnover at the top of our industry and the few elite leadership positions in the middle, the odds of a student climbing through the ranks are daunting. However, given those odds, carefully assessing the choices of current CEOs must stand as an absolute.

As another academic year comes to an end, we can only hope our students have been learning from these leaders. That they are reading their blogs, inspecting their websites, reading their trade publications, dissecting their speeches and ultimately following and analyzing their decisions.

To that end, our generous graduation gift to them could be this simple piece of advice: Leadership looks great at the top, but the secrets start at the bottom. Be a sponge and soak up everything.

49

Failing to Prepare Athletes for Lifestyle Only Feeds Problem

Published April 25, 2011

AS EDUCATORS OF STUDENT ATHLETES, we've long known what many league commissioners, team owners, and general managers think about every year after the annual league draft: Newfound affluence is an enormous challenge for young professional athletes.

That's because "making the show" often exposes a number of undeveloped life skills. It's most evident when a draftee is pushed from a protective collegiate environment into an often lonely first professional season.

The specters of fiscal mismanagement, rising debt, shady investments and lack of attention to earnings can converge on a 22-year-old and hang a financial albatross around his neck. Newfound friends, social popularity and back-slapping entourages are exciting and ego-building, but they also drain bank accounts and threaten statistical performance.

Many teams take the approach that it's not their responsibility to help young players manage personal finances. After all, lottery picks probably earn more than the general manager and can afford the finest investment advisers. The problem with this approach is that the

10. The Syracuse football team takes the field for a game at Metlife Stadium. *Courtesy of Syracuse University Athletics.*

general manger knows certain young players have never been around money and haven't enjoyed the luxury of positive financial influences.

Worse, the draftee may not know how to sustain a privileged life-style because he's never seen a checkbook or mastered the most basic tenets of personal accounting. In these situations, it's no surprise that many athletes find by the time they report to camp, they've already run up six-figure debt and made the decision to trust someone else to solve their problems.

Does Dez Bryant's plight ring a bell for you? The second-year Dallas Cowboys wide receiver (who, as a rookie, picked up a veteran player's dinner tab of almost $55,000 after refusing to carry teammate Roy Williams' pads during training camp) faces a lawsuit accusing him of owing a Texas-based jeweler nearly $600,000 for merchandise, tickets and loans. A separate lawsuit over $246,000 in jewelry was recently settled, according to media reports. Maybe he'll settle both lawsuits, but at what cost? And what's the real issue here?

Well, where individual fiscal failure harms a team most is evident in the player's emerging personal psychology. A player facing sudden or massive debt is more stressed and less mentally strong because no one is paying the pipers. To resolve this, many athletes turn to agents or someone in a trusted inner circle.

As the athlete abdicates financial control and ignores improper accounting or basic auditing, nervous or naïve behavior emerges. It makes young athletes susceptible to an increasing number of poor choices where they overlook their personal "burn rate." From there, a vicious cycle kicks in that can often lead to financial mismanagement, debt, drug use, alcoholism, unplanned children with multiple partners, eating disorders and/or expensive divorces.

Naturally, assisting players is a delicate business, and teams and leagues vary on how to help players learn money management. The NFL has previously offered a finance session during the league's rookie symposium. But in light of the NFL's current lockout and ongoing legal developments, it's worth asking whether the fiscal protection of young athletes should now be part of the league's next collective-bargaining agreement. Should the NFLPA include this concept in their demands of the owners? Should the owners include mandatory participation by players in a money management program as part of their demands?

The statistics of failure are not mythic. *Sports Illustrated* noted in 2009 that "by the time they have been retired for two years, 78 percent of former NFL players have gone bankrupt or are under financial stress because of joblessness or divorce." Likewise, "within five years of retirement, an estimated 60 percent of former NBA players are broke."

We believe every sports organization investing massive sums in college graduates should consider providing comprehensive ways of introducing basic money management concepts, including controlling one's financial affairs. If nothing else, we believe allowing players to think much more proactively about protecting earnings and guaranteeing substantial future income is good business.

There is no great secret to wealth management. The problem exists when individuals who have never been exposed to affluence must suddenly deal with a new lifestyle. For a team to fail to offer simple financial counseling is to subliminally play a role in the development of a problem that will return to haunt it when victories are on the line.

Most of us shake our heads in wonder when we read about players who earned $50 million and are now broke. Or read about star athletes found dead in back allies after seeking drugs. We shake our heads but rarely ask what early career initiatives could have prevented that fall from grace.

A 2009 article by *Business Pundit* listed 25 wealthy athletes who went broke. Guys like NFL running back Deuce McAllister, who turned a $70 million career into a $6 million debt in just a few years. Other examples include the NFL's Travis Henry, who fathered nine children by nine women and reportedly lost $20 million in the process.

To that end, the creation of some simple "master" classes by teams or life skills classes while athletes are still in school (we teach one at Syracuse) could easily provide simple financial counseling that requires no investment by the player and no pitches from financial services organizations. These classes could include life skills (e.g., safe sex, recognizing addictive behavior, etc.) as well as financial management strategies.

The benefit of higher education is more often than not to prepare citizens for a productive future and teach them to never stop learning. Pro teams might view entry-level fiscal education as an important employee-training program that picks up where college left off.

50

Why Lacrosse's Popularity Is Spreading across the U.S.

Published May 31, 2010

THE NCAA is scheduled to crown its 2010 Division I men's lacrosse champion today. Sadly for us, Syracuse University's bid to capture its third straight men's title was dashed in the first round of the tournament by Army. This year's women's NCAA champion, meanwhile, was slated to have been crowned on Sunday.

Given these concurrent dates, our upstate New York location (standing hard in the box-lacrosse-playing shadow of the Six Nations of the Iroquois) and our Canadian heritage, we decided it was time we wrote about the growth of lacrosse.

Known as Canada's national summer game, lacrosse represents one of the few NCAA major sports categories in which Ivy League schools like Cornell, Princeton, Brown and Yale can run comfortably with (and score on) the big boys from Syracuse, Notre Dame, North Carolina and Ohio State.

In the fast-growing women's game, which is played with slightly different rules from the men's game, blue-chip schools from Virginia, Northwestern and Stanford are commonplace near the top of the NCAA's rankings.

Finally, at the pro level, the Major League Lacrosse (the outdoor version of the men's college game) and National Lacrosse League (the pro version of box lacrosse, also known as indoor lacrosse) have both shown stability and staying power in the competitive sports entertainment world.

Setting those facts aside, what's more interesting is the astounding, almost exponential growth of the participation levels in this team game, invented by the original people of the land. Like a fast-spreading prairie fire, we can easily predict this sport has the surging capacity to emerge as a future revenue challenger to the other grass-based sports that North Americans cherish. We're not the only ones watching lacrosse: In a recent survey of 60 sporting goods industry experts, half picked lacrosse as the sport most likely to generate sales growth, according to the Sporting Goods Manufacturing Association's *State of the Industry Report.*

How interesting is it then that we might see North Americans return to their original athletic roots to play the oldest and formerly most popular game on the continent? And rather than read about a sport's owners and players threatening a strike or lockout, this sport is springing back to life with little concern for the haphazard U.S. economy or competitive initiatives of far larger league-driven games.

That's nice to write, but we certainly recognize that suburban participation doesn't necessarily equate to high-performance TV ratings and blanket avidity. Soccer, with its massive youth participation numbers in the United States and Canada, continues to trail the NFL, NBA, NHL and MLB at the professional level.

Lacrosse Growth

In fall 2009, the sport finance course at Syracuse was built around a project in lacrosse. Among the facts the students uncovered:

• Participation in U.S. high school lacrosse grew **528** percent between 1990 and 2008, as per the National Federation of State High School Associations.

• In 2007, it was estimated, by a survey authorized by the National Sporting Goods Association, that 1.2 million Americans older than age 7 had played lacrosse.

• By recent accounts, there are more than 240 men's and more than 300 women's college lacrosse teams playing in Division I, II and III.

• US Lacrosse reports suggested that in 2009, total lacrosse participation included more than 520,000 players, an increase of 8.4 percent from 2008 and more than double the 2001 number.

• An estimated 265,000 of those players were youths. US Lacrosse membership numbers (those players who are registered) hit 296,743 in 2008, a growth rate of 579 percent since the organization's inception in 1998.

Jim MacKenzie, the integrated marketing manager at New Balance Team Sports, which includes lacrosse brands such as Warrior and Brine, told us that lacrosse is "the growth sport for team sports in North America."

"The speed and strategies of the game and how the game is played matches up great with the other sports American kids are playing," he said. "Lacrosse has elements of football and ice hockey as well as the constant movement of soccer. It's natural in the spring for kids to move over to lacrosse. And playing lacrosse lets a young person carry their identity with them. Their stick is a part of who they are. Kids can bring their individual personalities to the game and it's really encouraged. Size and shape don't really matter."

So, in taking the input of the student research and MacKenzie's expertise, plus some of our own knowledge, we took a crack at attributing the growth drivers for lacrosse, and potentially for other sports.

1. Lacrosse has an original history and a devout following that is busting out of its original niche markets like Syracuse, Long Island and Baltimore.

2. Lacrosse is generally a high-scoring game that is played and enjoyed by both men and women. Plus, it sets up easily on a football or soccer field.

3. Lacrosse is a relatively easy game to learn and understand. Ball in the net equals one goal. Running, dodging, throwing, catching and shooting are frequent actions.

4. Lacrosse can be played in a low-cost way. True, the full competition game requires a helmet/eye guard and some padding, but recreationally, other than the stick and a ball, the game can be played on any piece of grass with two makeshift nets. A decent game can be played with as few as six people, and two people can play a game of catch almost anywhere.

5. Lacrosse has caught the attention of big-time sports apparel and equipment companies, who are helping grow the game while extending their team businesses.

6. Lacrosse is benefiting NCAA athletic departments as they deal with the complexities of gender equality because it provides a large-number participant team sport for women.

Lacrosse has huge momentum behind it and is making notable moves to become a choice sport of the future. At Syracuse, this is obvious. It may soon be that way elsewhere as well.

Index

Rick Burton is the award-winning David B. Falk Distinguished Professor of Sport Management in Syracuse University's Falk College of Sport and Human Dynamics. He serves as the university's Faculty Athletics representative to the National Collegiate Athletic Association and Atlantic Coast Conference. He also operates the Burton Marketing Group, focusing on strategic brand management and sponsorship and consulting for several professional sports leagues. Prior to his appointment at Syracuse, Burton served as the chief marketing officer for the U.S. Olympic Committee for the Beijing 2008 Summer Olympics and was the commissioner of the Sydney-based Australian National Basketball League from 2003 to 2007. He has written for the *New York Times, Wall Street Journal, Ad Age, SportsBusiness Journal, SI.com, Sport Business International,* and *Stadia* and has hosted his own sports business television show. His first novel, a World War II/Cold War historical thriller titled *The Darkest Mission,* was published in May 2011 (www.thedarkestmission.com). He also coauthored the textbook *Global Sport Marketing: Sponsorship, Ambush Marketing, and the Olympic Games* (2015) with Norm O'Reilly, Richard Pound, Benoit Seguin, and Michelle Brunette. He and his wife, Barbara, have three children and live outside of Syracuse in New York's Finger Lakes region.

Norm O'Reilly is recognized as one of the leading scholars in the business of sports. He is the Richard P. and Joan S. Fox Professor of Business and chair of the Department of Sports Administration at Ohio University's College of Business. O'Reilly has expertise in a range of business topics, including analytics, marketing, sponsorship, social media, sport finance, social marketing, tourism management, and management education. He has authored or coauthored seven books, 14 case studies in the Harvard/Stanford series, and more than 90 peer-reviewed journal articles. His books include *Sports Business Management: Decision Making around the Globe* (with George Foster and Tony Davila, 2016) and *Global Sport Marketing: Sponsorship, Ambush Marketing, and the Olympic Games* (with Richard Pound, Rick Burton, Benoit Seguin, and Michelle Brunette, 2015). For nearly 10 years, he has been minority owner and senior adviser with the Consulting Group of Toronto marketing agency TrojanOne. He was a member of the 2004, 2008, and 2010 Mission Staff for the Canadian Olympic Committee at the Olympic Games. He and his wife, Nadege, live in picturesque Athens, Ohio, with their four children (Emma, Kian, Thomas, and Leland).